By RHODA HOFF

WHY THEY WROTE

Dickens
Thoreau
Flaubert

New York *HENRY Z. WALCK, INC.* 1961

LIBRARY OF CONGRESS CATALOG CARD NUMBER: 61-9956

PRINTED IN THE UNITED STATES OF AMERICA

CONTENTS

I CHARLES DICKENS
1812-1870

WHENEVER TALK TURNS to English literature, Charles Dickens is named as one of England's greatest men of letters. While he lived, his popularity was fantastic; when he died, he was mourned by a nation, rich and poor alike. Queen Victoria sent a personal message of sympathy to his family; a workingman, stopping in at a tobacconist's for a twist of tobacco, threw his money on the counter and said, "Charles Dickens is dead. We have lost our best friend." Now, almost a hundred years after his death, all the major Dickens novels are still in print. And not only are they on the library shelves, they still rank high in popular appeal. Charles Dickens was not a perfect writer. His books are loosely constructed, the writing is uneven, the characters often teeter on the verge of caricature. But Dickens possessed one quality that atoned for every technical lapse: he had genius.

And, knowing he had been given genius, he was willing to subordinate his life to its dictates: "I hold my inventive capacity on the stern condition that it must master my whole life, often have complete possession of me, make its own demands upon me, and sometimes, for months together, put everything else away from me,"

Dickens writes. "Whoever is devoted to an art must be content to deliver himself wholly up to it, and to find recompense in it."

But in spite of this devotion to his art, Charles Dickens loved life too much to pass it by. Vital, intense, moody, feverishly active and inordinately gifted, he had the energy, not only to service his genius, but to do enough living to satisfy an average man. Yet in spite of his great inventive gift, in spite of his full life as a man, Charles Dickens hunted restlessly, until he died, for something he could never find.

Night after night, a consuming restlessness drove him out onto the deserted London streets or sent him prowling the empty country lanes near his home at Gad's Hill. "Whatever it is, it is always driving me, and I cannot help it," he wrote his friend John Forster. "If I couldn't walk fast and far, I should just explode and perish." Perhaps the thing Charles Dickens never stopped searching for, the "whatever it is" he was unable to define, was a lost childhood. For from the time he was eleven years old, Dickens had no childhood at all.

Charles John Huffam Dickens was born in Landport, Portsea, on Friday, the 7th of February, 1812. His father, a clerk in the Navy pay office, was an easygoing, gay, companionable sort of man. Proud of his attractive young son, he loved to show him off, setting him up on a table when he was only four years old, and egging on the child, who already had a precocious flair for acting, to sing music hall songs for the entertainment of applauding friends and relatives.

When Charles was five, the family moved to Chatham, where they led a normal, middle-class life. Charles and his sister, Fanny, went to school with the other children; and, for a Sunday treat, Mr. Dickens would take his young son walking along the Rochester Road. High on a hill stood an impressive house known as Gad's

Hill Place. An aura of legend hung about Gad's Hill as the rendezvous of Shakespeare's Falstaff, and the house itself was the grandest in the neighborhood. With characteristic ambition, "the very queer small boy" called Charles Dickens at once conceived a desire to live there. His easygoing father gave him some advice he himself never saw fit to practice: "If you were to be very persevering and were to work hard," he told his son, "you might some day live in it." Eventually Charles Dickens did live at Gad's Hill Place; but between the dream and its fulfillment lay forty-odd years of intensive work, brilliant accomplishment and stormy living.

Until Charles was eleven this pleasant life at Chatham continued. Delicate and high-strung and now one of eight children, this "very-small-and-not-overly-particularly-taken-care-of boy" (as Dickens described himself later to Washington Irving), spent much of the time shut up alone in a small upstairs room where his father kept what he rather grandly called his library. It consisted, among other books, of *Tom Jones, The Vicar of Wakefield, Robinson Crusoe, Don Quixote* and *The Arabian Nights.* "They kept alive my fancy and my hope of something beyond the place and time," Dickens said. They also inspired him to do some writing of his own, and he became quite famous with his child-public at Chatham, especially for a tragedy called *Misnar, the Sultan of India,* a work that descended rather obviously from the Arabian Nights.

But the Chatham days came to a sudden and dramatic end, and Charles began to live in a nightmare, for the genial John Dickens was only a grown-up child when it came to money. Unable to resist anything that gave him pleasure, he overspent outrageously, piling up a load of debts he was unable to pay off. With his wife and his eight children, John Dickens fled to London where Mrs. Dickens dreamed a wild dream of staving off the ruin that was advancing on her family by opening a school for young ladies. A house was found, a brass plate reading "Mrs. Dickens's Establishment" was nailed to the door, and Charles, the eldest son, now just twelve, was sent out to distribute a sort of prospectus. "I left, at a great many doors, a great many circulars calling attention to the merits of the establishment. Yet nobody ever came to school. But I know that we got on very badly with the butcher and baker; that very often we had not too much for dinner; and that at last my father was arrested."

In 1824 John Dickens was sentenced to the Marshalsea debtors' prison, and for a while his family tried to carry on without him. They sold or pawned what possessions they still had. As the oldest son, Charles was entrusted with these business transactions. The beloved books were the first things to go. When there was nothing left to sell except a few chairs, a kitchen table and some beds, Mrs. Dickens gave up the struggle. With her youngest children she joined her husband inside the Marshalsea. Fanny, the oldest daughter, won a scholarship at the London School of Music, and Charles was sent to work in a blacking factory owned by a cousin of his mother's. As the factory was too far away from the prison for convenient commuting, Charles lived all alone in mean lodgings, supporting himself on his weekly wage of six shillings (about $1.50).

The blacking factory was in an old, tumble-down house on the river, overrun by rats. Together with two boys of about his own age, rough and uneducated companions in misery, the sensitive, highly-gifted young Charles pasted labels onto blacking bottles from morning till night. When he was finished at the factory he went back to his lonely lodgings, subsisting for the most part on bread and cheese, which he kept in his closet. "No words can express the secret agony of my soul," he wrote in a fragment of biography he suppressed until he died, "as I sunk into this companionship; compared these every-day associates with those of my earlier childhood;

and felt my early hopes of growing up to be a learned and distinguished man, crushed in my breast. The deep remembrance of the sense I had of being utterly neglected and hopeless; of the shame I felt in my position; of the misery it was to my young heart to believe that day by day, what I had learned and thought and delighted in and raised my fancy and my emulation up by, was passing away from me, never to be brought back any more, cannot be written."

His agony of frustration was made worse when he had to watch his sister Fanny win a prize at the Royal Academy of Music. "I could not bear to think of myself—beyond the reach of all such honorable emulation and success," he says. "The tears ran down my face. I prayed when I went to bed that night to be lifted out of the humiliation and neglect in which I was. I never had suffered so much before. There was no envy in this."

In the end John Dickens was bailed out of prison by a legacy from his mother. From this source he received enough money, not only to pay off his debts, but to start life modestly anew. The depressed period in the history of the Dickens family had lasted just under a year, but it was long enough to scar the sensitive Charles permanently. Worst of all, was that when his father came out of prison, Charles did not also gain his release from the blacking factory. It was only when his father quarreled with Charles's employer that the boy was rescued from his drudgery. And even then, Mrs. Dickens tried to patch things up between her husband and her cousin, so that the family would not be deprived of the six weekly shillings Charles earned. Dickens never cared for his mother after that. "I do not write resentfully or angrily," he said, looking back on that period, "for I know all these things have worked together to make me what I am but I never afterwards forgot, I never shall forget, I can never forget that my mother was warm for my being sent back."

Although Dickens always remained bitter about the blacking factory days, this experience did trigger some positive results. Even at twelve years of age, Charles Dickens had a seeing eye. Some of the most famous episodes in his books are built on the things he observed when he was an underprivileged boy visiting his father in prison, slaving in a sweatshop and wandering lonely and ill-fed through the meaner streets of London. Furthermore, that brutal year drove iron into the soul of Charles Dickens. Revolting against the futility of his easygoing parents, Charles learned an important lesson at an early age: either you work to better your life or you remain submerged forever. Dickens chose to work. He worked when he was a boy, he worked when he was a young man; he worked, as he himself said, "with a celestial or diabolical energy" all his life long until he exhausted his never very robust health and died, largely from overwork, at the age of fifty-eight. "Do everything at your best," he urged his own children. "I can truly assure you that I have taken as great pains with the smallest thing I have ever undertaken as with the biggest."

Released from the blacking factory, Charles was at last sent to school. But the experience came too late to be of much benefit. Wellington House Academy, as the school was called, was a mediocre place, and Dickens only stayed there a little over two years. One of his classmates describes him as a "handsome, curly-haired lad, full of animation and animal spirits" who wrote stories which were circulated among the boys. Charles took part in all the schoolboy pranks and was a leader at building small theaters and giving plays. But schoolboy pranks, schoolboy theatricals and schoolboy literary activities were rather insipid fare for a boy who had seen as much of the grim side of life and suffered as Charles Dickens had. He was just fifteen when he left school to take a job as clerk with a Gray's Inn solicitor at a salary of fifteen shillings a week. He was glad to be out in the world.

In later years, when people asked John Dickens about his famous son's education, even that easygoing parent was forced to hem and haw: "Why, indeed, sir—ha! ha!" he would confess, "he may be said to have educated himself!"

It was not long before Charles Dickens had decided that he was not interested in the study of law and that, therefore, he was wasting his time at Gray's Inn. And he was in no mood to waste time for he had fallen passionately in love with Maria Beadnell, the daughter of a bank manager. Maria was pretty and coquettish and she alternately encouraged and spurned her suitor. Dickens's social position was no match for Maria's, and her parents did everything they could to break up the affair. But the relationship went on for four years, and, in an attempt to prove to Maria's parents that he was a worthy husband for their daughter, Dickens was spurred on to make a name for himself. Twenty-three years later, looking back on this passionate, youthful romance, Dickens wrote, "It excluded every other idea from my mind for four years, at a time of life when four years are equal to four times four; I went at it with a determination to overcome all the difficulties, which fairly lifted me up into that newspaper life, and floated me away over a hundred men's heads." To Maria herself, when both of them were middle-aged, he wrote, "It is a matter of perfect certainty to me that I began to fight my way out of poverty and obscurity, with one perpetual idea of you."

Maria may have provided the immediate incentive, but it was the Dickens character, his ambition, optimism and fortitude, which in the end lifted him out of poverty and obscurity. Strangely enough, the key to escape was handed to him by his father, who had become fascinated by a new skill called shorthand. Although no longer a young man, John Dickens mastered the difficult technique with surprising rapidity and went on to a job as parliamentary reporter for a newspaper.

Hearing that many distinguished young men had begun their rise to success as parliamentary reporters, Charles decided to follow his father's example. He bought himself one of the new shorthand manuals and set to work, slaving through the nights because he was holding down a full-time job during the day. And dedicated as he was to self-improvement as a means to winning Maria, he also spent long hours at the library catching up on the education that had been denied him. It was a strenuous program, but all his life Charles Dickens was a strenuous man.

In 1832, at the age of nineteen, he gave up his job at the solicitor's office and set forth to look for work in his new field. He found it, first as reporter for a law office, then as parliamentary reporter on the staff of the *Morning Chronicle.* "There never *was* such a shorthand writer," says a colleague.

Maria Beadnell's parents succeeded at last in breaking up the romance between the young people; but the work Dickens had chosen as the shortest path to success for her sake suited his restless, driving nature. A star reporter, he was soon being sent all over the country to cover the news for his paper. "There never was anybody connected with newspapers, who, in the same space of time, had so much express and post-chaise experience as I," Dickens reminisced in later years. These were still the old coaching days, picturesque and romantic but extremely uncomfortable. "I have often transcribed for the printer, from my short-hand notes, important public speeches," Dickens tells us, "in which the strictest accuracy was required and a mistake in which would have been to a young man severely compromising, writing in the palm of my hand, by the light of a dark lantern, in a post-chaise and four, galloping through a wild country and through the dead of the night, at the surprising rate of fifteen miles an hour."

It was an exhausting life but it was also a rewarding one. And it was the best possible training ground for an embryo writer. With its emphasis on accurate observation and clear writing, journalism laid the foundation for Dickens's future work as an author. "To the wholesome training of severe newspaper work, when I was a very young man, I constantly refer my first successes," Dickens told some New York editors when he was on a visit to America.

Those "successes" were not long in coming. Alert, quick-witted and hard-working, Charles Dickens was not satisfied for long with his role of reporter. He began, in addition to his other work, to write short stories. One of these, "A Dinner at Poplar Walk," seemed to him good enough to be printed. He sent it off to a magazine. It was promptly accepted. Dickens was overcome with emotion when, for the first time, he saw himself a published writer. "I walked down to Westminster Hall," he says, "and turned into it for half an hour, because my eyes were so dimmed with joy and pride that they could not bear the street and were not fit to be seen there." The story appeared in the *Old Monthly* magazine in December, 1833. Dickens was twenty-one years old.

As the *Old Monthly* was, at the time, in the financial doldrums, Dickens received no pay for his work. Nevertheless, it seemed wonderful to him to be a printed author and, always a facile writer, he tossed off another eight stories, signing them, according to the fashion of the day, with a pseudonym. The name he chose was "Boz." It was a nickname he had given his youngest brother; "Moses," from *The Vicar of Wakefield,* pronounced through the nose, became Boses and then, for the sake of brevity, Boz.

In time, however, glory was not enough for the poor and struggling young Dickens—he wanted to be paid for his work. The *Morn-*

ing Chronicle, his own paper, had just started an evening version, the *Evening Chronicle,* and Dickens persuaded them to commission him to write some "light papers," in addition to his regular reportorial assignments, and to raise his salary for the package deal from five to seven guineas a week.

The man who acted as intermediary in this transaction was George Hogarth, the music editor. Hogarth was a man of culture and refinement. He had an attractive house as well as three charming daughters, Catherine, nineteen, Mary, fifteen and Georgina, seven. The brilliant and talented Charles Dickens was soon a regular visitor to the Hogarth home. The three girls made a great fuss over the attractive young man, and Dickens reciprocated by loving all three girls at once. But Catherine, the oldest daughter, was the only one of marriageable age, and soon she and Charles Dickens had become engaged. There was a long delay between engagement and marriage, however, because Charles Dickens was not yet able to support a wife.

But soon this impediment was removed. The stories Dickens had written for the *Old Monthly* and the *Evening Chronicle* had not proved sensational, but they had enjoyed a mild popular success. What was more important, they had attracted the attention of a firm of publishers, Chapman and Hall. Humorous and humanly interesting, the sketches by Boz were a novelty in their day. For instead of indulging in the extravagant romanticism then popular, they told of everyday people leading everyday lives. These first Dickens stories displayed the precision of observation and the descriptive power which later made him famous. At any rate Chapman and Hall liked the stories well enough to ask their author to undertake a modest writing job for them. One of the well-known humorous artists of the day, Robert Seymour, had agreed to do a series of comic drawings centering around the adventures of a group of amateur sportsmen and their Nimrod Club. Originally, all Dickens was asked to do was to write what was called the "letter-press," really no more than glorified captions to be used as an ornamental border surrounding the drawings. But neither publisher nor artist had correctly estimated the power of that young go-getter, Charles Dickens. Forceful, determined and persuasive he succeeded in reversing the role of writer and artist. This is the story as he himself tells it: "The idea propounded to me was that the monthly should be a vehicle for certain plates to be executed by Mr. Seymour; and there was a notion, either on the part of that admirable humorous artist or of my visitor [the publisher] that a Nimrod Club, the members of which were to go out shooting, fishing and so forth, would be the best means of introducing these." On the grounds that he was "no great sportsman" and that, in any case, the idea was a trite one, Dickens persuaded his employers that "it would be infinitely better for the plates to arise naturally out of the text: and that I would like to take my own way, with a freer range of English scenes and people."

As *The Pickwick Papers,* edited by Boz, the story appeared in monthly installments beginning April, 1836, and ending November, 1837. Beginning without much success, the serial had become a best seller by the time its fourth installment came off the press. Seymour, a depressed type of man, had committed suicide, but another artist was found and Pickwick continued his triumphant journey. Mr. Pickwick enjoyed a renown that produced a rash of "Pickwick" coats (dark green or plum with large brass buttons), "Pickwick" hats, "Pickwick" gaiters and even a cigar known as the "Penny Pickwick."

Even before Pickwick had reached the printed page, Dickens had sold the copyright of the sketches by Boz for 150 pounds. With cash in his pocket and good prospects in the offing, Charles Dickens and Catherine Hogarth were married on the 2nd of April, 1836. They spent their honeymoon at an inn between Gravesend and Rochester, the country that Dickens had loved as a child and to which he remained loyal all his life. Returning to London, they settled in modestly at Dickens's old bachelor quarters in Furnival Inn, which was not a tavern but a sort of apartment house. An American visitor calling on Dickens there reported finding the young author in an "uncarpeted and bleak-looking room with a deal table, two or three chairs and a few books."

But notwithstanding his simple way of life, Dickens had already become something of a celebrity. In book form, *Pickwick* was a bonanza. "If I were to live a hundred years, and write three novels in each," said the jubilant Dickens, "I should never be so proud of any of them as I am of *Pickwick,* feeling as I do, that it has made its own way, and hoping, as I must own I do hope that long after my hand is withered as the pens it held, *Pickwick* will be found on many a dusty shelf with many a better work."

Dickens was not just a literary genius, he was also a man of action, and he set to writing one book after another with the prodigality of genius and the drive of a tycoon. Everyone wanted to meet the new literary sensation and almost everyone did. Carlyle, coming home from a dinner with Dickens, reported that, "He is a fine little fellow Boz, I think. Clear, blue intelligent eyes, eyebrows that he arches, amazingly large, protrusive mouth, a face of most extreme mobility, which he shuttles about—eyebrows, eyes, mouth and all—in a very singular manner while speaking." But Charles Dickens's face was not always mobile; he had learned to use his elbows in hard times, and there was always a hard side to his nature. Mrs. Carlyle, always an astute observer, noticed this at once: "He has a face made of steel," she said.

On the 6th of January, 1837, Charles Dickens, Jr., the first of the ten Dickens children, was born. The proud father wanted his son to have a better start than he had, so Dickens decided to move into what he called a "frightfully first class Family Mansion."

Dickens was now twenty-five. Fame and fortune were his, he had a wife, a son and a beautiful new home; the world was his oyster. Then suddenly tragedy struck. Before the birth of little Charles, Mary Hogarth had come to live with her sister. She was a young girl of sixteen, sweet and remote, and endowed with an exceptionally charming and gentle nature. When the Dickenses moved to the new house, nobody wanted to part with Mary, so she came along, permanently one of the family. One night Dickens took his wife and Mary to the theater. Mary seemed in fine health and spirits. But when they reached home she was suddenly taken ill. She died the next day. "Thank God she died in my arms," Dickens wrote a friend, "and the very last words she whispered were of me. . . . I solemnly believe that so perfect a creature never breathed. I knew her inmost heart, and her real worth and values. She had not a fault."

Brooding over the girl's death, Dickens came to feel that Mary Hogarth had been the prototype of ideal womanhood. Her death affected him so deeply he was unable to write a word for two months. Even *Pickwick* could not wean him from his grief, and publication had to be interrupted. Six years after Mary's death, Dickens was still grieving. "After she died, I dreamed of her every night for many months," he wrote her mother, "sometimes as a spirit, sometimes as a living creature, always with a kind of quiet happiness, which became so pleasant to me that I never lay down at night without a hope of the vision coming back in one shape or another." Being a writer, Dickens possessed the means to make his vision of Mary live again. He resurrected her as the young, sweet, perfect heroine of his books. She was Little Nell in *The Old Curiosity Shop* and Agnes in *David Copperfield.*

In time the youngest sister, Georgina, substituted for the dead Mary. Georgina was a sensible, plain spinster; she remained with Dickens until he died; and, as Catherine was an impractical woman, it was Georgina who managed the house and children and took over the care of the babies. In his will Dickens called her "the best and truest friend man ever had." But all that was many years in the future. And for Charles Dickens it was the present that was important. *Pickwick* came to a triumphant conclusion, and immediately Dickens began a new novel. As his first book had been comedy, he decided to show off another facet of his talent in his second story.

In 1837 the spirit of radicalism was sweeping through the world. Dickens was caught up in the current, more especially as his own deprived childhood had given him a firsthand experience of the seamy side of life. Identifying himself with the injustices and the inequities of the social scene, he became the champion of reform: reform in education, reform in prison laws, reform in the field of child labor. The new book, *Oliver Twist,* with its pathetic orphan hero, its grim pictures of the workhouse and its picture of the underworld, was the first of the Dickens social novels. Fascinated by the writing of it, Dickens begrudged every moment he had to take from his work. On a much-needed vacation with his wife and baby, he wrote his friend, John Forster, "I have had great difficulty in keeping my hands off Fagin and the rest of them in the evenings; but I came down for rest, I have resisted the temptation and steadily applied myself to the labor of being idle."

All his life long, idleness was the hardest labor of all for Charles Dickens. Success sent commissions pouring in, and with restless zeal he set himself to doing the work of three men. *Nicholas Nickleby* was begun before *Oliver Twist* was concluded and a new serial,

Barnaby Rudge, was contracted for. Three books at the same time proved too much even for a writer of Dickens's energy and virtuosity, and he wrote Forster that he had the sense of "something hanging over him like a hideous nightmare." With Forster's help, *Barnaby Rudge* was postponed. But that still left *Oliver Twist* and *Nicholas Nickleby,* both appearing serially, so that each month Dickens had to produce two separate installments of two different novels.

Serialization imposes certain unavoidable difficulties on the writer. In addition to planning his novel as a whole, he must provide each installment with some sort of climax and he must tailor his monthly contributions to approximately the same size. If a novel is finished before it is serialized, the work as a whole does not suffer. But anxious as he was for fame and monetary success, Dickens could never wait till he completed a novel before he offered it for serialization. As soon as he had enough material on hand to fill four or five numbers, he rushed into print. By the time he was halfway through his book, even this modest head start had usually dwindled to a one-installment lead. Each number of *Nicholas Nickleby,* for instance, according to Dickens himself, was completed "only a day or two before its publication." No wonder that his work suffers from a certain diffuseness, giving the impression at times that it has been hastily improvised; no wonder that sometimes his characters undergo some rather capricious changes between the beginning of a story and its end. Mr. Pickwick, for instance, who started out as something of a buffoon, evolves into a lovable, sentimental old gentleman by the time the story is finished.

Added to the drawbacks unavoidable in this sort of hurried writing was the need Dickens felt to please his large and vocal audience. Often readers wrote the author while his story was still being constructed, making known to him their wishes concerning their favorite characters. Dickens could, of course, have paid no attention;

but, craving popularity and success as he did, he sometimes gave in to the whims of his public. In writing the character of Walter Gay in *Dombey and Son,* Dickens refrained from portraying him as he had first planned, as "travelling away from that love of adventure and boyish lightheartedness, into negligence, idleness, dissipation, dishonesty and ruin," because he was afraid it might disappoint some of his fans. "Do you think it may be done, without making people angry?" he nervously inquires of Forster. And when Lord Lytton objected to the sad ending designed for *Great Expectations,* Dickens obliged with a happy conclusion.

It was this lack of firm construction in Dickens's books as well as their somewhat capricious manipulation of character which led his great contemporary, Gustave Flaubert, a man who was dedicated to art, to say of Dickens: "How little he cares for art!"

But in spite of their faults, Dickens's books live with a curious intensity: they are not so much lifelike as they *are* life. Dickens's craftsmanship may at times be poor, his plotting too reliant on the "happy coincidence"; it doesn't matter. To make up for these technical lapses, Dickens has a devastating vitality, an insatiable love of life and a talent for expressing warmth that make his books incomparable companions.

This vitality and deep love of living surged up from the depths of his nature and gave his personal life a feverish activity. Endowed with an amazingly creative imagination and a prodigious capacity for work, Dickens was unbelievably fertile. By the time he was thirty, he had written seven novels in addition to many short stories and plays. He had already fathered four children (in the end there were ten) and he had made many warm friends. A man of seemingly limitless energy, he wanted to do everything at once and to do everyone's work as well as his own. At home he patrolled his house each morning to see that the shades were drawn to the exact spot he thought fitting and that each chair was in its correct place; he supervised the decoration of his daughters' rooms, told the younger children stories, nursed the sick ones, and was the leader in all the family games.

But his writing occupied the major portion of his time. All his life he worked long hours, always under pressure. "I worked pretty well last night, very well indeed; but although I did eleven close slips [pages] before half-past twelve I have four to write to close the chapter." Or again, "I was working incessantly until it was time to dress and have not yet got the subject of my last chapter which must be finished to-night." But there were times, even for Dickens, when inspiration waned, and he would describe himself as "sitting at home waiting for Oliver Twist who has not yet arrived." And sometimes it would be, "I could not write a line till three o'clock and have yet five slips to finish."

But as he worked his way deeper and deeper into his stories, his characters became so real to him that he rejoiced and suffered with them as they lived out their fictional lives. The death of Little Nell was almost as sad to him as if she had been a real child: "I think [this part of the story] will come famously," he wrote Forster, "but I am the wretchedest of the wretched. It casts the most horrible shadow upon me, and it is as much as I can do to keep it moving at all. I tremble to approach the place. . . . Nobody will miss her like I shall. It is such a very painful thing to me, that I really cannot express my sorrow." Dickens's child characters were especially dear to him, and Paul Dombey's death was just as painful to him as Little Nell's: "He died on Friday night at 10 o'clock," he wrote a friend, "and as I had no hope of getting to sleep after-wards, I went out, and walked about Paris until breakfast-time next morning." But even small happenings in his books were so vivid to him that his senses reacted as if the events he was describing were actually true. When writing about the prison riots in *Barnaby Rudge,* Dickens says, "Another number will finish the fires, and help us towards the end. I feel quite smoky when I am at work."

With *David Copperfield,* Dickens reached the height of his genius, although his fame and popularity continued to grow until he died. *David Copperfield* began its serial run in May, 1848, and in 1850 the story was published in book form. It was Dickens's favorite novel: "Like all fathers," he said, "I have a favorite child and his name is *David Copperfield.*" Writers are known to be poor judges of their own books, but, in Dickens's case, critics and public alike endorsed his choice. This story about a poor boy whose miserable childhood is modeled on Dickens's own youthful suffering was in its essence more of a passionate biography than a work of fiction. By creating the hero of his new novel in his own image, Dickens was forced to relive the painful memories connected with his blacking factory days. In addition to airing his own childhood troubles, he was also able to give fulfillment to his half-unconscious love for Mary Hogarth by creating the character of Agnes, the perfect wife, in her image. Dickens understood his own "case," and he spoke of his "so happy and yet so unhappy existence which seeks its realities in unrealities, and found its dangerous comfort in a perpetual escape from the disappointment of heart around it."

No wonder he was sorry when he neared the end of *David Copperfield:* "I am within a few pages of the shore," he wrote Forster, "and am strangely divided, as usual in such cases, between sorrow and joy. If I were to say half of what Copperfield makes me feel to-night, I should be turned inside out! I seem to be sending some part of myself into the shadowy world."

Writing for the first time of characters and events inspired by life as he himself had experienced it, Dickens left behind him the fantastic, heightened atmosphere of his earlier novels and entered a more realistic world. From now on, his novels achieved a new level of excellence. The books of this second period have been judged his finest work; with them he achieved world fame and was acclaimed one of the great novelists of all time. His popularity in America was as great as in his own country and even on the continent he was widely read in translation.

The boy who began life in such humble circumstances seemed now to have inherited the earth. But Dickens was feeling the results of his long years of strain and feverish work. He was tired. The waning of creative power increased the restlessness from which he had always suffered to some extent until it reached morbid proportions. "Still the victim of an intolerable restlessness," he wrote John Forster. "I shouldn't be at all surprised if I wrote you one of these mornings from under Mont Blanc. I sit down between whiles to think of a new story and, as it begins to grow, such a torment of a desire to be anywhere but where I am; and to be going I don't know where I don't know why; takes hold of me, that it is like being *driven away.*"

In writing *David Copperfield,* Dickens had been forced to probe into his life and to recognize that he was deeply unhappy with his wife. For a while he took out his longing for a more fulfilling life in escape of every kind—escape in traveling, escape in every kind of distraction, but especially escape through work. In addition to his novel writing, he now plunged into amateur theatricals and gave readings for charity from his books. For a long time he had been thinking of editing a magazine that would feature the best contemporary fiction and also run interesting articles on science, politics and social problems. Beginning March 1, 1850, he realized this ambition, acting as editor in chief of a new periodical called *Household Words.* He took his editorial duties seriously. He went to his office almost every day, read manuscripts, edited them, and corresponded with the authors. As Dickens was not a man who enjoyed talking about his own writing, these letters of editorial advice give the best picture we have of Dickens's ideas on his art and his methods of work. "I can give you no better counsel," he wrote one young author, "than to look into the life about you and to strive for what is noblest and true."

On another contributor he urges patience: "I have no means of knowing whether you are patient in the pursuit of this art; but I was inclined to think that you are not, and that you do not discipline yourself enough. When one is impelled to write this or that, one has still to consider: 'How much of this will tell what I mean? How much of it is my own wild emotion and superfluous energy—how much remains that is truly belonging to this ideal character and these ideal circumstances?' It is in this laborious struggle to make this distinction, and in the determination to try for it, that the road to the correction of faults lies. Perhaps I may remark, in support of the sincerity with which I write this, that I am an impatient and impulsive person myself, but that it has been for many years the constant effort of my life to practise at my desk what I write to you."

In 1858, Dickens separated from his wife of twenty-two years. The underlying cause undoubtedly was a deep incompatibility. "Poor Catherine and I are not made for each other, and there is no help for it," he wrote Forster. "It is not only that she makes me uneasy and unhappy but that I make her so too—and much more so. . . . We are strangely ill assorted for the bond there is between us. Her temperament will not go with mine." All this was no doubt true, but it had been true for a long time. The difference now was that Dickens had met a young actress during some amateur theatricals and had fallen in love with her. This was the immediate cause of a separation which shocked the whole of England. All his writing life Dickens had sung the praises of family life and married love so that his defection caused widespread dismay. But Dickens was far too intense to be deterred by criticism in this case.

Shortly before the break with his wife, the place at Gad's Hill, which Dickens had admired so enviously as a boy, was put up for sale. Dickens bought it in 1857, and in 1858 he sold his London house and moved to the country permanently. He remained at Gad's Hill until his death.

In order to pay for the house and also to assuage his terrible restlessness, Dickens now decided to give for his own benefit the readings from his novels which he had, from time to time, given in support of some charity. From 1858 until his death in 1870, he made four of these tours, editing, altering and adapting his material for this new purpose.

As a lecturer, Charles Dickens was an unqualified success. In their enthusiasm, his audiences behaved as if they were at a revival meeting. They laughed, they cried, they went into ecstasies, they had hysterics. Dickens loved it all. Sometimes, in their enthusiasm, the audience would rush the hall, pouring into the auditorium until confusion reigned. "I read with the platform crammed with people," Dickens reported after such a night. "I got them to lie down on it, and it was like some impossible tableau or gigantic picnic—one pretty girl in full dress, lying on her side all night, holding on to one of the legs of my table! It was the most extraordinary sight. And yet from the moment I began to the moment of my leaving off, they never missed a point, and they ended with a burst of cheers."

To an author who of necessity must write in solitude, this tangible fame was a heart-warming experience. And financially the reading tours were immensely rewarding. But the constant excitement, the incessant traveling and the late hours were physically damaging. "I seem always to be either in a railway carriage or reading or going to bed," Dickens said. To get an idea of the physical strain the readings imposed on Dickens, one has only to cite one medical fact. With an ordinary pulse of 72, Dickens had a pulse of 114 when reading *Dombey,* a pulse of 124 when reciting *The Mystery of Edwin Drood.* Nor were the lecture trips his entire life. He was still editing a magazine, still working at his novels. *A Tale of Two Cities, Great Expectations, Our Mutual Friend* and the half-finished *Edwin Drood* were the fruit of these late years. But overwork, overstrain and overexcitement left their mark, and these last books are not considered his best work.

There was something tragic in Dickens's last, driven, restless years. During the time of his humiliation in the blacking factory, the twelve-year-old boy had decided that for those who have strong will power, everything is possible. Now the tired, unhappy man, feeling his creative powers waning, tortured by the failure of his marriage and the demands of late love, made a desperate attempt to force a way through his difficulties by forcing his energy and will power to the breaking point. But there is a limit to what will power can accomplish: "I can force myself to go aboard a ship," Dickens said, "and I can force myself to do at that reading desk what I have done a hundred times; but whether, with all this unsettled, fluctuating distress in my mind, I could force an original book out of it, is another question."

Dickens did what he could. In 1867 he got aboard a ship and went to America to give a strenuous tour of readings. By the end of the trip he was on the verge of collapse. He recovered somewhat on the sea voyage home, went back to Gad's Hill for some rest, then began a new reading tour in England. After a few appearances, even this man of strong will and relentless energy saw that he could no longer stand the pace. He was unable to sleep, unable to see clearly; he dragged his left foot, and his memory became uncertain. His doctors insisted that he cancel the rest of the tour. On March 15, 1870, in London, Dickens made his farewell appearance. Stepping up to the footlights at the end of his performance, he said: "From these garish lights I vanish now forevermore, with a heartfelt, grateful, respectful, affectionate farewell."

Home again at Gad's Hill, he went to work on *Edwin Drood* and was relieved to see that in its first monthly number the work sold 50,000 copies. His genius was still pulling strong. Writing in the little Swiss Chalet he had set up in his garden, Dickens enjoyed his last spring: "I have put five mirrors in the Swiss Chalet where I write, and they reflect and refract all kinds of ways the leaves that are quivering at the window. My room is up among the branches of the trees; and the birds and the butterflies fly in and out, and the lights and shadows of the clouds come and go with the rest of the company. The scent of the flowers, and indeed of everything that is growing for miles and miles is most delicious."

On June 8, he worked in the Chalet all day. Toward evening he left off and went back to the house to dine with his sister-in-law, Georgina Hogarth, who had remained with him even after the departure of her sister. Suddenly Dickens began to talk incoherently and fell to the ground unconscious. He had suffered a paralytic stroke, and he died the next day.

England reacted to the death of her most loved novelist as if the country had suffered a national disaster. Writing of his death, the London *Times* said: "It will be felt by millions as nothing less than a personal bereavement." This was the kind of tribute Charles Dickens would have liked. For in the last analysis it is the warmth and friendliness of his genius which has given him his unique place in literature. Champion of the poor and poet of the commonplace, he was a force in history as well as a great writer. His books did much to gain better conditions for working children. They helped to lessen the brutality in English schools, and they aided in abolishing the debtors' prison. And as an artist, Dickens created a world peopled with characters so real that they were "company" for thousands of people who lived with them, shared their joys and sorrows, and counted them as friends.

Charles Dickens was buried in Westminster Abbey with England's greatest men. And on the gravestone of this writer who could use words superlatively well, is chiseled an inscription so unadorned that it is arresting by its very simplicity:

CHARLES DICKENS
Born February the Seventh, 1812
Died June the Ninth, 1870

FROM THE POSTHUMOUS PAPERS OF THE PICKWICK CLUB BY CHARLES DICKENS

Mr. Pickwick found that his three companions had risen, and were waiting his arrival to commence breakfast, which was ready laid in tempting display. They sat down to the meal; and broiled ham, eggs, tea, coffee, and sundries, began to disappear with a rapidity which at once bore testimony to the excellence of the fare, and the appetites of its consumers.

"Now, about Manor Farm," said Mr. Pickwick. "How shall we go?"

"We had better consult the waiter, perhaps," said Mr. Tupman, and the waiter was summoned accordingly.

"Dingley Dell, gentlemen—fifteen miles, gentlemen—cross road —post-chase, sir?"

"Post-chase won't hold more than two," said Mr. Pickwick.

"True, sir—beg your pardon, sir. Very nice four-wheel chaise, sir—seat for two behind—one in front for the gentleman that drives—oh! beg your pardon, sir—that'll only hold three."

"What's to be done?" said Mr. Snodgrass.

"Perhaps one of the gentlemen like to ride, sir," suggested the waiter, looking towards Mr. Winkle; "very good saddle horse, sir—any of Mr. Wardle's men coming to Rochester, bring 'em back, sir."

"The very thing," said Mr. Pickwick. "Winkle, will you go on horseback?"

Now Mr. Winkle did entertain considerable misgivings in the very lowest recesses of his own heart, relative to his equestrian skill; but, as he would not have them even suspected on any account, he at once replied with great hardihood, "Certainly. I should enjoy it, of all things."

Mr. Winkle had rushed upon his fate; there was no resource. "Let them be at the door by eleven," said Mr. Pickwick.

"Very well, sir," replied the waiter.

The waiter retired; the breakfast concluded; and the travellers ascended to their respective bed-rooms, to prepare a change of clothing, to take with them on their approaching expedition.

Mr. Pickwick had made his preliminary arrangements, and was looking over the coffee-room blinds at the passengers in the street, when the waiter entered, and announced that the chaise was ready—an announcement which the vehicle itself confirmed, by forthwith appearing before the coffee-room blinds aforesaid.

It was a curious little green box on four wheels, with a low place like a wine-bin for two behind, and an elevated perch for one in front, drawn by an immense brown horse, displaying great symmetry of bone. An hostler stood near, holding by the bridle another immense horse—apparently a near relative of the animal in the chaise—ready saddled for Mr. Winkle.

"Bless my soul!" said Mr. Pickwick, as they stood upon the

pavement while the coats were being put in. "Bless my soul! who's to drive? I never thought of that."

"Oh! you, of course," said Mr. Tupman.

"Of course," said Mr. Snodgrass.

"I!" exclaimed Mr. Pickwick.

"Not the slightest fear, sir," interposed the hostler. "Warrant him quiet, sir; a hinfant in arms might drive him."

"He don't shy, does he?" inquired Mr. Pickwick.

"Shy, sir?—he wouldn't shy if he was to meet a vaggin-load of monkeys, with their tails burnt off."

The last recommendation was indisputable. Mr. Tupman and Mr. Snodgrass got into the bin; Mr. Pickwick ascended to his perch, and deposited his feet on a floor-clothed shelf, erected beneath it, for that purpose.

"Now, shiny Villiam," said the hostler to the deputy hostler, "give the gen'lm'n the ribbins." "Shiny Villiam"—so called, probably, from his sleek hair and oily countenance—placed the reins in Mr. Pickwick's left hand; and the upper hostler thrust a whip into his right.

"Wo—o!" cried Mr. Pickwick, as the tall quadruped evinced a decided inclination to back into the coffee-room window.

"Wo—o!" echoed Mr. Tupman and Mr. Snodgrass, from the bin.

"Only his playfulness, gen'lm'n," said the head hostler, encouragingly; "jist kitch hold on him, Villiam." The deputy restrained the animal's impetuosity, and the principal ran to assist Mr. Winkle in mounting!

"T'other side, sir, if you please."

"Blowed if the gen'lm'n worn't a gettin' up on the wrong side," whispered a grinning post-boy to the inexpressibly gratified waiter.

Mr. Winkle, thus instructed, climbed into his saddle, with

about as much difficulty as he would have experienced in getting up the side of a first-rate man-of-war.

"All right?" inquired Mr. Pickwick, with an inward presentiment that it was all wrong.

"All right," replied Mr. Winkle, faintly.

"Let 'em go," cried the hostler—"hold him in, sir"; and away went the chaise, and the saddle horse, with Mr. Pickwick on the box of the one, and Mr. Winkle on the back of the other, to the delight and gratification of the whole inn yard.

"What makes him go sideways?" said Mr. Snodgrass, in the bin, to Mr. Winkle, in the saddle.

"I can't imagine," replied Mr. Winkle. His horse was drifting up the street in the most mysterious manner—side first, with his head towards one side of the way, and his tail towards the other.

Mr. Pickwick had no leisure to observe either this, or any other particular, the whole of his faculties being concentrated in the management of the animal attached to the chaise, who displayed various peculiarities, highly interesting to a by-stander, but by no means equally amusing to any one seated behind him. Besides constantly jerking his head up, in a very unpleasant and uncomfortable manner, and tugging at the reins to an extent which rendered it a matter of great difficulty for Mr. Pickwick to hold them, he had a singular propensity for darting suddenly every now and then to the side of the road, then stopping short, and then rushing forward for some minutes, at a speed which it was wholly impossible to control.

"What *can* he mean by this?" said Mr. Snodgrass, when the horse had executed this manoeuvre for the twentieth time.

"I don't know," replied Mr. Tupman; "it *looks* very like shying, don't it?" Mr. Snodgrass was about to reply, when he was interrupted by a shout from Mr. Pickwick.

"Woo," said that gentleman, "I have dropped my whip."

"Winkle," cried Mr. Snodgrass, as the equestrian came trotting up on the tall horse, with his hat over his ears: and shaking all over, as if he would shake to pieces, with the violence of the exercise. "Pick up the whip, there's a good fellow." Mr. Winkle pulled at the bridle of the tall horse till he was black in the face; and having at length succeeded in stopping him, dismounted, handed the whip to Mr. Pickwick, and, grasping the reins, prepared to remount.

Now, whether the tall horse, in the natural playfulness of his disposition, was desirous of having a little innocent recreation with Mr. Winkle, or whether it occurred to him that he could perform the journey as much to his own satisfaction without a rider as with one, are points upon which we can arrive at no definite and distinct conclusion. By whatever motives the animal was actuated, certain it is that Mr. Winkle had no sooner touched the reins, than he slipped them over his head, and darted backward to their full length.

"Poor fellow," said Mr. Winkle, soothingly—"poor fellow—good old horse." The "poor fellow" was proof against flattery: the more Mr. Winkle tried to get nearer him, the more he sidled away; and, notwithstanding all kinds of coaxing and wheedling, there were Mr. Winkle and the good old horse going round and round each other for ten minutes; at the end of which time, each was at precisely the same distance from the other as when they first commenced—an unsatisfactory sort of thing under any circumstances, but particularly so in a lonely road, where no assistance can be procured.

"What am I to do?" shouted Mr. Winkle, after the dodging had been prolonged for a considerable time. "What am I to do? I can't get on him."

"You had better lead him till we come to a turnpike," replied Mr. Pickwick, from the chaise.

"But he won't come," roared Mr. Winkle. "Do come and hold him."

Mr. Pickwick was the impersonation of kindness and humanity; he threw the reins on the horse's back, and having descended from his seat, carefully drew the chaise into the hedge, lest anything should come along the road, and stepped back to the assistance of his distressed companion, leaving Mr. Tupman and Mr. Snodgrass in the vehicle.

The horse no sooner beheld Mr. Pickwick advancing towards him with the chaise whip in his hand, than he exchanged the rotatory motion in which he had previously indulged for a retrograde movement of so very determined a character, that it at once drew Mr. Winkle, who was still at the end of the bridle, at a rather quicker rate than fast walking, in the direction from which they had just come. Mr. Pickwick ran to his assistance, but the faster Mr. Pickwick ran forward, the faster the horse ran backward.

There was a great scraping of feet, and kicking up of the dust; and at last Mr. Winkle, his arms being nearly pulled out of their sockets, fairly let go his hold. The horse paused, stared, shook his head, turned round, and quietly trotted home to Rochester, leaving Mr. Winkle and Mr. Pickwick gazing on each other with countenances of blank dismay. A rattling noise at a little distance attracted their attention. They looked up.

"Bless my soul!" exclaimed the agonized Mr. Pickwick, "there's the other horse running away!"

It was but too true. The animal was startled by the noise, and the reins were on his back. The result may be guessed. He tore off with the four-wheeled chaise behind him, and Mr. Tupman and Mr. Snodgrass in the four-wheeled chaise. The heat was a short one. Mr. Tupman threw himself into the hedge, and Mr. Snodgrass followed his example, the horse dashed the four-wheeled chaise against a wooden bridge, separated the wheels from the body, and the bin from the perch; and finally stood stock still to gaze upon the ruin he had made.

The first care of the two unspilt friends was to extricate their unfortunate companions from their bed of quickset—a process which gave them the unspeakable satisfaction of discovering that they had sustained no injury, beyond sundry rents in their garments, and various lacerations from the brambles. The next thing to be done was, to unharness the horse. This complicated process having been effected, the party walked slowly forward, leading the horse among them, and abandoning the chaise to its fate.

II HENRY DAVID THOREAU
1817-1862

HENRY DAVID THOREAU was born in Concord, Massachusetts, on July 12, 1817; he died in Concord only forty-five years later. Except for four years as a Harvard undergraduate and a few short trips to Cape Cod, to the Maine woods, to New York, and once, shortly before he died, as far West as the upper reaches of the Mississippi, Thoreau's entire world was bounded by one small New England town. Yet neither as a man nor as a writer did he feel the need for a wider horizon. "Wherever men have lived there is a story to be told," he says, "and it depends chiefly on the story-teller whether that is interesting or not. . . . You are simply a witness on the stand to tell what you know about your neighbors and your neighborhood."

Thoreau proved to be an incomparable witness. At once a naturalist and a poet, he saw with equal clarity the "outer" world of sense and perception and the "inner" world of thought. "I wish to live ever as to derive my satisfaction and inspirations from the commonest events, so that what my senses hourly perceive, my daily walk, the conversations of my neighbors, may inspire me, and I may dream of no heaven but that which lies about me," he writes in one mood. But in another he says, "Explore your higher latitudes. . . .

Nay be a Columbus to whole new continents and worlds within you, opening new channels, not of trade but of thought."

Thoreau never wrote of anything he had not, himself, seen or experienced. *Walden,* one of the great books of American literature and one of the handful of American classics to win international fame, is a report, written in simple and noble prose, on one man's experiment in woodland living and one man's search for reality in himself and nature. In his essay, "Civil Disobedience," Thoreau writes of his own resistance to a government he could not believe in because of its weak stand against slavery, a government he fought armed only with passive resistance. What he had to say out of his own deep conviction held so much universal truth that it inspired Gandhi to fight his own crusade against the government of India by non-violent means.

But Thoreau is not so much a builder of books as a master of the isolated and luminous thought. He is at his best in the journals he began when he was twenty-one and which he continued to write as long as he lived. "I do not know," he says, "but thoughts written down in a journal might be printed in the same form with greater advantage than if the related ones were brought together in separate essays. . . . The crystal never sparkles more brightly than in the cavern. How will you rivet them together without showing the mark of the file?" For Thoreau, his journals were a bank of thoughts and observations on which he drew when writing his books and lectures. In the lifelong conversation with himself which these diaries represent, he explores his neighborhood, his neighbors and his own "higher latitudes" with equal integrity and equal clarity of observation. It is this double vision, this passionate adventuring in both the material and immaterial worlds, which gives Thoreau's work its unique appeal.

Henry David Thoreau was born in his grandmother's home in

Concord village, "an old-fashioned house with a roof nearly reaching to the ground in the rear." But from the time he could walk, a house was of little interest to him. He loved the out of doors. "In the country a boy's love is likely to be divided between a gun and a watch," he wrote as a man, "but the more active and manly choose the gun." The young Thoreau was no precocious boy-naturalist; he chose the gun, as most of his playmates did. He was different from the other boys in only one respect: his senses were so acute that he could hear and see things to which most of us must remain deaf and blind. "His power of observation seemed to indicate additional senses," Emerson says. "He saw as with microscope, heard as with ear-trumpet, and his memory was a photographic register of all he heard."

From long days spent in the woods or on the river, Thoreau came home at night to an affectionate and congenial family circle. There was John Thoreau, the silent, hard-working father who began life as a prosperous storekeeper, lost his money, and made a fresh start at Concord manufacturing lead pencils. There was Cynthia Thoreau, Henry's mother, the real manager of the family, energetic, ambitious, and as talkative as her husband was silent. In addition to Henry, there were three other children: John, the oldest son, the only Thoreau who found it easy to make friends; and the two girls, the intellectual Helen, and Sophia, the baby of the family, an awkward, plain girl who hero-worshiped her brother Henry as long as he lived. With the world of nature at his front door and a happy home to return to at night, Henry led an enchanted childhood. "I think that no experience which I have to-day comes up to, or is comparable, with the experience of my boyhood," he wrote when he was a man. "My life was ecstasy."

Henry was seventeen when he graduated from Concord Academy and entered Harvard. Although the whole family contributed to send him to college, he still had so little money that he had to go to chapel in a green, homespun coat when everyone else was wearing conventional black and white. He was a good student but not a brilliant one. For some reason he took few science courses, concentrating instead on the classics and modern languages. His mind was highly original and creative and was not at its best when imprisoned in the academic format. Henry Thoreau never felt that he had been taught anything of great value at Harvard. Some years after his graduation, when he heard Emerson telling a young man that Harvard taught all branches of learning, he commented wryly, "All the branches and none of the roots."

What promise Thoreau showed at college was as a scholar rather than as a writer. A young man who believed that "knowledge does not come to us by details but in flashes of light from heaven" could not but be impatient with the training in logic, organization and discipline of mind which the Harvard curriculum offered. "What I was learning in college was chiefly, I think, to express myself," Thoreau wrote a boy who was Harvard-bound, six years after his own graduation, "and I see now that my teachers should have prescribed to me: 1st, sincerity; 2nd, sincerity; 3rd, sincerity." But sincerity was something which Henry Thoreau was very well equipped to teach himself, while a feeling for accuracy and discipline in thought and expression, which he was taught, is a good tool for any writer to have and one which Thoreau undoubtedly found useful in perfecting his vigorous and terse style.

In 1837, when Henry Thoreau arrived home after graduating from Harvard, his family, for reasons of economy, had moved into the house of John Thoreau's sister. In addition to her brother's family, Miss Thoreau had another boarder, Mrs. Lucy Jackson Brown, a sister-in-law of Emerson's. Mrs. Brown was some years older than Henry, but she was charming, and lonely because her husband had gone abroad on business for a long stay. She and the young Harvard graduate became great friends, a relationship which, on Henry's side at any rate, developed sentimental overtones. Romantic and intense, he picked bunches of flowers for his friend, wrote verses to go with them, and tossed his offering in at her window in true young-poet style. One of his poems said:

> I am a parcel of vain strivings tied
> By a chance bond together
> Dangling this way and that. . . .

This was better truth than poetry. For at this period, Henry Thoreau *was* a "parcel of vain strivings." He wanted to be a writer but he had to earn his living, and he was clear-sighted enough to know that his writing had not yet reached the stage where it could support him. He faced the problem all young creative artists must face, but in his case it was aggravated by a craving for leisure. "A broad margin of leisure is as beautiful in a man's life as in a book," he writes.

Leisure, however, has to be earned, and at twenty-one Thoreau was not yet eligible to lead a life of quiet contemplation. After some indecision, he solved his problem by deciding to teach, and he got a job teaching in Concord's elementary school. He was full of admiration for the new theories on education which Bronson Alcott had been trying out in Boston, and he determined to put them into practice at Concord. As soon as he met his class, he announced that he "should not flog, but would talk morals as a punishment instead." This was all very fine and idealistic but it ignored the unhappy fact that the Concord school board was still in the "spare the rod spoil the child" stage of thinking. It was only a short while before the young teacher was in open conflict with his superiors. Ordered to flog, Thoreau did so, but in his own way. Choosing six victims at random, he flogged the good with the bad, thus showing his contempt of authority and holding the issue up to ridicule. Having done this, he very wisely handed in his resignation. It was promptly accepted.

Thoreau's next venture into teaching was more successful. With his brother, John, he opened a school of his own, teaching classics and mathematics while John took over all the executive work. Today we would call the school which the Thoreau brothers ran "progressive." It was a happy, relaxed place, which, in addition to the regular curriculum, featured long walks, trips on the river and cross-country treasure hunts for arrowheads and wild flowers. Henry's schedule left him plenty of free time for reading, thinking and tramping. The school was a success from the beginning, and there were more pupils than could be accommodated. But in 1840, John's health began to fail (he died two years later), and the school was closed.

Meanwhile Henry had met Emerson, who had come to live in Concord a few years before. During the Harvard years, Henry had read Emerson's essay, "Nature," and had been deeply influenced by it; now, he too began to keep a journal. A mutual friend showed the journal to Emerson, and a friendship that was to last a lifetime was born. From the very first, Emerson recognized the latent power in this young, forthright, talented boy and called him "*the* man of Concord." In his journal he wrote, "I delight much in my young friend, who seems to have as free and erect a mind as any I have ever seen."

Nathaniel Hawthorne, who had also come to live in Concord, was another person who saw the "singular character behind the rough exterior." In his journal he wrote, "A young man with much of the wild, original Nature still remaining in him. He is a keen and delicate observer which I suspect is almost as rare a character as even an original poet. And Nature, in return for his love, seems to adopt him as her especial child; and shows him secrets which few others are allowed to witness. . . . With all this he has more than a tincture of literature; a deep and full taste for poetry, especially for the elder poets; and he is a good writer." Mrs. Hawthorne called this Pan of Concord, "life-inspired."

But the school had closed down, and Henry Thoreau did not know what he should do next. "Be resolutely and faithfully what you are," he advised himself in his diary. "Be sure you give men the best of your wares though they be poor enough, and the gods will help you to lay up a better store for the future." For a while Emerson watched from the sidelines. "At this time, a strong healthy youth, fresh from college," he says about Henry Thoreau. "Whilst all his companions were choosing their profession, or eager to begin some lucrative employment, it was inevitable that his thoughts should be exercised on the same question, and it required rare decision to refuse all the accustomed paths and keep his solitary freedom at the cost of disappointing the natural expectations of his family and friends; all the more difficult that he had a perfect probity." The farmers and shopkeepers who were Henry's neighbors at Concord were beginning to call him an "oddity" and a ne'er-do-well. But genius has a way of recognizing genius, and Emerson decided to give this young idealist a helping hand. He asked him to come and live in the Emerson home and be a sort of combined friend, handy man, caretaker, baby-sitter and companion to Mrs. Emerson when her husband had to be away on lecture tours. As Emerson put it, Henry was to "receive bed and board in exchange for what he chooses to do."

Henry accepted the job with alacrity. At this time Emerson was already a famous man and a leader of American intellectual life. At his house the most brilliant men and women of the day met for talk and stimulating companionship. In the Emerson home, Thoreau could converse informally with men and women like Nathaniel Hawthorne, Bronson Alcott, Margaret Fuller, a pioneer in the woman's movement, and Elizabeth Peabody, Hawthorne's sister-in-law, whose Boston bookstore was the meeting place for all the young intellectuals of the town. Dreamers and idealists, these people differed from each other in many ways but they were united in a search for the spiritual truth that lies behind all appearance. "Inspiration" and "intuition," they believed, were the keys to this kingdom. This ardent and talented group of New England men and women are called "transcendentalists," but they themselves used no label. Independent, thoughtful and austere, Henry Thoreau could not have found a more congenial environment in which to develop his talent.

Thoreau lived in Emerson's home from 1841 to 1843. At this time Emerson was preaching that the chief function of a writer is to "report life"—first of all his own life. And Henry Thoreau, heavily under the master's influence, set himself to doing just this. But he enlarged the Emerson directive to include both the writer's thoughts and his environment. Although he conscientiously mowed the Emerson lawn, played with the Emerson children, and helped with all the odd jobs around the house, Thoreau had plenty of free time to tramp the countryside and observe the flora and fauna around him. In the evenings he would struggle to put what he had seen and heard and thought into fitting words. It was a difficult task, but in the end Thoreau was able to write about nature with an accuracy of observation, an almost organic identification and a poetic insight that make his descriptions unforgettable: "I saw a distant river by moonlight," he writes, "making no noise, yet flowing, as by day, still to the sea, like melted silver reflecting the moonlight." Or, at another season, "The thin snow now driving from the north and lodging on my coat consists of those beautiful star crystals, not cottony and chubby spokes, but thick and partly transparent crystals. They are about a tenth of an inch in diameter, perfect little wheels with six spokes without a tire, or rather with six perfect little leaflets, fern-like, with a distinct straight and slender main-rib, raying from the centre." When spring came he was inspired to a prose that was in reality poetry. "The grass flames up on the hill-sides like a spring fire—as if the earth sent forth an inward heat to greet the returning sun; not yellow but green is the color of its flame. . . ." Summer, autumn, winter or spring, each in its own way was beautiful, its magic intensified for Henry Thoreau by a pantheism that endowed all nature with cosmic meaning: "These motions everywhere in nature must be the circulations of God."

But during these youthful years, although Henry Thoreau could see and hear and enjoy with a rich intensity, he was not yet able to write as well as he thought. Coming home from his long walks through wood and swamp and meadow, he would search out Emerson and try to learn from him how to express in fitting language what he had seen. "Henry Thoreau's conversation [at this time] consisted of a continual coining of the present moment into a sentence and offering it to me," Emerson remarked. Behind the controlled words there is a note of irritation; obviously it was disturbing to Emerson's peace to have his disciple living at such close quarters.

If the relationship between master and disciple was sometimes strained, Thoreau's friendship with Emerson's wife was happy and rewarding. Lidian Emerson, fifteen years older than her house guest, was a shy, witty, frail woman who, because of her husband's lofty and remote nature, was often lonely. She and Henry Thoreau became good companions, and in 1842, when Lidian's little son died and Thoreau lost his brother John the same year, the bond between them became very strong. Henry Thoreau had been in love a few years before with a young girl, Ellen Sewall. He had written a letter of proposal to her and been turned down, partly because her conservative family had disapproved of a "transcendentalist," but that short romance was nothing more than a youthful episode. But at twenty-five Thoreau was capable of a more lasting emotion, and he became deeply attached to Lidian Emerson. Lidian, however, was a married woman, so he sublimated his feeling for her and gave her a vague, uplifted, transcendental-type emotion in which love was a sort of friendship and friendship a sort of love.

For two years Thoreau lived in Emerson's house working and thinking and practicing his writing in articles and poems. Some of these had been published in the *Dial,* a magazine founded by Emerson and Margaret Fuller with the dual objective of offering an outlet to the young writers who were Emerson's disciples and at the same time serving as the voice of transcendentalism. Thoreau had also followed Emerson to the lecture platform. He was, however, a poor lecturer and although he continued to lecture at intervals as long as he lived, he always talked above the heads of his audience and could never wean himself away from reading from a prepared manuscript. "After lecturing twice this winter," Thoreau wrote in 1853, "I feel that I am in danger of cheapening myself by trying to become a successful lecturer, i.e. to interest my audiences. I am disappointed to find that most that I am and value myself for is lost, or worse than lost, on my audiences. I fail to get even the attention of the mass. I should suit them better if I suited myself less. I feel that the public demand an average man—average thoughts and manners—not originality, not even absolute excellence. "Thoreau could never fit himself into the mold of the average man, and what was true in 1853 was even more true in the apprentice days of 1842. Lecturing could certainly not be counted on as a means of earning a living.

Writing paid even less, for the *Dial* offered its writers only the glory of appearing in print, and Thoreau's philosophical type of writing was far removed from what the ordinary magazine of the day was prepared to publish. Nor could Thoreau stay on forever, mowing Emerson's lawn and doing his odd jobs. The time had very definitely come for him to make an effort to earn a steady income. Once more Emerson came to the rescue. He secured for his protégé a job as tutor to his brother William's son. The William Emersons lived on Staten Island, and the hope was that, in addition to tutoring his pupil, Thoreau would have time to go to New York, establish contacts there with editors and publishers, and perhaps discover some market for his literary wares. So, buttressed with a fine collection of letters of introduction provided by the faithful Emerson, Thoreau set out on his Staten Island adventure.

With his first earnings he bought himself a new pair of trousers (they cost $2.50) and journeyed to New York. He presented his letters of introduction to Henry James, Horace Greeley and the journalist, Brisbane; he visited the editorial offices of six magazines. But, as he reported to Emerson, only one of these, the *Ladies Home Companion,* paid its contributors, and, said Thoreau, "I could not write anything companionable."

Thoreau had done his best. Conscientiously, he had made the uncongenial rounds, but he could find no place for his writings in the commercial market. Unsuccessful, depressed and physically unwell, he became very homesick. "Methinks I should be content to sit at the back door in Concord, under the poplar tree, henceforth forever," he wrote his mother.

He stuck it out on Staten Island for just six months. Then he returned to Concord. This time he lived with his family, lending his father a hand in building a new house so far from the center of town that the Thoreaus christened it "Texas." Henry also helped out in the family business, making pencils that were better than any then in use. He even went to Boston to exhibit his product and obtain certificates of excellence from various chemists and artists. He got the endorsements he wanted, but when his friends at Concord congratulated him Thoreau said that he would never make another pencil. "Why should I?" he asked. "I would not do again what I have done once." He did, however, invent a new process for making graphite which eventually proved so successful that John Thoreau, some years later, was able to give up pencil-making entirely and to devote himself to the new venture, which made him quite prosperous.

Meanwhile Thoreau had been doing some hard thinking. He had tried schoolteaching, magazine writing and lecturing, and all of these attempts at earning money had proved to be either uncongenial or unprofitable or both. Evidently money making was not compatible with a temperament that demanded plenty of leisure and the opportunity to live out of doors. The only solution to the problem was to live so simply that the need for money would be reduced to a bare minimum. "What you call bareness and poverty is to me simplicity," he told a friend who did not approve of the new idea. "In proportion as a man simplifies his life, the laws of the universe will appear less complex and solitude will not be solitude, nor poverty poverty." What irreducible wants might still remain could be satisfied by a few odd hours of manual labor.

But even this type of simple living was not easy to come by. "I am led about from sunrise to sunset by an ignoble routine and yet can find no better road," Thoreau complained, until once again Emerson intervened to save the day. He had just acquired a field of eleven acres and a lot of four acres on the shore of Walden Pond, a few miles outside of Concord village, and he suggested to Thoreau that he go there to live. Thoreau accepted the suggestion but, as usual, he insisted on paying his way by offering to clear a large piece of ground for his landlord and planting it with young pines. It was a fair exchange.

"I lived alone, in the woods, a mile from any neighbor," Thoreau writes in *Walden,* his most famous book, "in a house which I built myself, on the shore of Walden Pond, in Concord, Massachusetts, and earned my living by the labor of my hands only. I lived there two years and two months." More of a hut than a house, Thoreau's residence cost him exactly twenty-eight dollars and twelve and one half cents. It was money well spent. It bought peace of mind and the material for a book which is considered one of the masterpieces of literature.

According to William Ellery Channing, a close friend, Thoreau's cabin on the shores of Walden Pond was "just large enough for one . . . a sentry box on the shore, in the wood of Walden, ready to walk into in rain or snow or cold. . . . By standing on a chair you could reach into the garret, and a corn broom fathomed the depth of the cellar. It had no lock to the door, no curtain to the window, and belonged to nature as much as to man."

Here Thoreau began his famous experiment in simple living. He raised beans and potatoes for food and accepted a few odd jobs and a little surveying to satisfy the rest of his Spartan needs. When this small amount of work was done, he owned his days. They were spent in exploring the world of nature, in contemplation, in writing a book, and in reading.

It was at Walden that Thoreau first discovered the *Bhagavad-Gita,* and the great Hindu poem was so congenial to his nature that it crystallized his thinking. Arjuna, the hero of the *Bhagavad-Gita,* succeeds in freeing himself from personal attachments and personal wants and so is enabled to fix his soul on the Eternal. "He who is content with wisdom and clear-seeing, who is victorious over the senses, to whom a piece of dirt, a piece of stone, a piece of gold are all equal is established in the Rule," says the *Bhagavad-Gita.* "Let the man of the Rule hold himself always under the Rule, remaining in seclusion, utterly subdued in mind, without cravings and without possessions." Thoreau set himself to living by the Rule. "All I can say," he declares, "is that I live and breathe and have my thoughts."

To Emerson, looking on from the outside, Thoreau seemed to be turning into the "great renouncer." But one man's meat is another man's poison, and Thoreau was happier at Walden than he had been since his boyhood. For him there was one great positive which made up for all the negatives, and that was the world of nature. To Thoreau, nature was more than trees and woodchucks and the fish in Walden Pond; it was first and foremost the "means and symbol" of something bigger. "The other world is all my art," he said; "my pencils will draw no other; my jack-knife will cut nothing else."

In the peace of his retreat at Walden, Thoreau wrote his first full-length book, *A Week on the Concord and Merrimack Rivers.* Together with his brother, John, Thoreau had spent a happy week on those rivers six years earlier. Henry had, as always, kept a journal during the seven days the two brothers had floated down the rivers in a boat they had made themselves. Much of the material for *The Week* was supplied by this journal, but the factual record was padded liberally with quotations, philosophy and nature observations. Unless the word "travel" is expanded to include not only a river trip but a voyage through Thoreau's mind, *The Week* is not a travel book.

Although Thoreau lived alone during the time he was at Walden, he was not the hermit he has been pictured. Walden Pond was only a few miles from Concord, and the villagers, especially during the summer months, often trekked out to visit Henry, who received them in his pine grove when the weather permitted. In fact, as Thoreau's aunt wrote a friend, "going to see Henry became one of Concord's best recreations."

Often, too, Thoreau walked into town to visit his family and friends and to do errands. On one of these jaunts he was imprisoned for refusing to pay a poll tax to a government he did not approve of because of its weak stand against slavery. He was only in jail overnight (a friend paid his tax for him the following morning); but the episode is important because it spurred Thoreau on to write his essay, "Civil Disobedience," in which he says that "that government is best which governs least."

On September 6, 1847, Thoreau shut up his hut at Walden and returned to Concord. The experiment he had begun two years earlier had proved a success. He had lived by the work of his hands; he had written a book; and he had clarified his personal philosophy. Enriched and fortified, he returned home, ready to look in a new direction. People have often wondered why Thoreau did not stay longer at Walden. Thoreau answers that question in his journal. "Perhaps it seemed to me," he says, "that I had several lives to live and could not spare any more time for that one." It was characteristic of Henry Thoreau that, having extracted from an experience what it had to teach, he turned his attention to something new. "Not till we are lost, in other words not till we have lost the world do we begin to find ourselves," he writes, "and the infinite extent of our relations." In the solitude of Walden Pond he had found himself; now he wanted to express this new self in a fresh contact with people.

This was the underlying reason for Thoreau's return to Concord. The immediate reason was that Emerson was going abroad for a year and once more Lidian and the Emerson children were in need of a friend and protector. So Thoreau moved from his cabin in the woods to Emerson's home. Six years had passed since his last visit. He was now a man of thirty, a writer who had completed one book and had started another. Once more he and Lidian kept house together and once more the friendship that was between them brought warmth into both their lives. "Lidian and I make good housekeepers," Thoreau wrote Emerson. "She is a very dear sister to me." And if the word "sister" was a little too gentle to express Thoreau's feelings for his benefactor's wife, outwardly, at any rate, the relationship between the stay-at-homes conformed to the name Thoreau gave it. But in his journal Thoreau told what "a sister" meant to him: "One in whom you have unbounded faith —whom you can purely love. . . . A gentle spirit—a wise spirit—a loving spirit. An enlargement to my being. . . ." Many people have said that Thoreau was a cool and passionless man. This is not true. There is no doubt that, in his own way, he loved Lidian Emerson.

In 1848 Emerson came home, and Thoreau went to live again with his own family. Except for a few short trips, he never left either them or Concord again. And he was glad of the fact that his life was confined in this narrow channel. "I cannot but regard it as a kindness in those who have the steering of me," he says, "that, by the want of pecuniary wealth, I have been nailed down to this my native region so long and steadily, and made to study and love this spot of earth more and more. What would signify in comparison a thin and diffused love and knowledge of the whole world instead, got by wandering?"

The success of the graphite business had made the Thoreaus comfortable, and Henry felt justified in taking permanent refuge under the family roof. All he needed now was pocket money. As his wants were few, he could satisfy them easily by taking a few odd jobs and by acting as the town surveyor. In 1847 he wrote a humorous description of his doings for his Harvard class book: "I am a Schoolmaster, a private Tutor, a Surveyor, a Gardener, a Farmer, a Painter, I mean a House Painter, a Carpenter, a Mason, a Day Laborer, a Pencil Maker, a Writer & sometimes a Poetaster." A collection of half truths; but to his journal he confided the basic truth: "My work is writing, and I do not hesitate, though I know that no subject is too trivial for me, tried by ordinary standards; for ye fools, the theme is nothing, the life is everything, all that interests the reader is the depth and intensity of the life excited." Not even Thoreau's worst enemy could have denied that he was an intense man who lived his life in depth. "Thoreau was sincerity itself," Emerson says, "and might fortify the conviction of prophets in the ethical laws by his holy living."

The first thing Henry tried to do after his return to Concord, was to arrange for the publication of *The Week*. Emerson tried to help, but in spite of his recommendation four publishers turned the book down. It was finally published at the author's expense, six years after it was written. Thoreau said that he "was obliged to manufacture a thousand dollars worth of pencils and slowly dispose of and finally sacrifice them," in order to pay off his debt to his publishers. In spite of the loyal support which its author's distinguished friends gave the book, *The Week* received only the mildest praise from the critics, while the reading public ignored its existence completely. In 1853 the publishers returned the unsold books to their author, 706 out of an edition of 1,000 copies. "They have arrived to-day by express," Thoreau noted in his journal. "I have now a library of nearly nine hundred volumes over seven hundred of which I wrote myself."

As soon as Thoreau had returned to Concord from Walden Pond, he had begun to write the story of his experiment in simple living. *Walden, or Life in the Woods,* as the book was called, went the rounds of the publishers, and again Thoreau had to wait six years before his work finally appeared in print. This time, however, the firm of Tichenor and Fields paid the bill.

In essence *Walden* is one of the first "how-to" books. It tells how to purge your life of everything that is not essential, then earn the money to satisfy your simplified wants by working with your hands. In our own day, when the craving for material things has become something of an American obsession, Thoreau's solution to living is more timely than ever before. And because, in addition to being a philosopher and a man of action, Thoreau is also a poet and a naturalist, *Walden* appeals equally to the dreamer, the doer and the nature-lover. "I learned this at least by my experiment," Thoreau says in this passionate autobiography, "that if one advances confidently in the direction of his dreams, and endeavors to live the life which he has imagined, he will meet with a success unexpected in his common hours. . . . If you have built castles in the air, your work need not be lost; that is where they should be. Now put the foundations under them."

These are ringing words; they are also practical words. Above all, they are words that are characteristic of Henry Thoreau. All his life long, in the face of poverty and discouragement, the poet in him dreamed and marveled while the builder patiently laid the foundations to support the dreams. "Surely joy is the condition of life," says Thoreau, the poet. "Think of the young fry that leap in ponds, the myriad of insects ushered into being in a summer evening, the incessant note of the hyla. . . ." Then the realistic Thoreau speaks. "Man is the artificer of his own happiness. Let him beware how he complains of the disposition of circumstances, for it is his own disposition he blames."

Walden sold two thousand copies and was very well received by the critics. This success came at an opportune time, for the six years of waiting had not been easy ones for Thoreau. Seemingly, he had been doing nothing, and his Concord neighbors had begun to think of him as an idler, a harmless do-nothing who would never amount to anything. Even Emerson had wavered in his faith. In his journal of July, 1851, he had written, "Thoreau wants a little ambition in his mixture. Fault of this instead of being the head of American engineers, he is Captain of a Huckleberry party."

Thoreau himself had not the least desire to be the "head of American engineers." He had only one ambition: "It is a great art in the writer to improve from day to day just that soil and fertility which he has," he wrote in his journal, "to harvest that crop which his life yields, whatever it may be, not be straining as if to reach apples or oranges when he yields only ground-nuts." So, ignoring the judgments people passed on him, he kept his eye on his goal and went steadfastly on his way. From the time he returned to live with his family in 1848, until he died in 1862, his daily life followed one simple pattern. With the exception of the very few odd-job and surveying days during which he earned the money for his simple needs, Thoreau never deviated from his routine. In the mornings he read, wrote and studied; in the afternoons he took walks; in the evenings he copied into his journal the facts he had observed on his walks and the thoughts they had brought him. From the outside, looking in, it sounds like a dull life; but, as Thoreau said, "The art of life, of a poet's life, is not having anything to do, to do something."

The long walks through wood and swamp and meadow usually lasted three to four hours and were the heart of Thoreau's day. As he grew older, Thoreau attracted many young men who believed that this manly and able naturalist with the searching, "terrible" eyes was "the man of men," the guide who could tell them how they should live their own lives. They begged to be allowed to accompany him on his walks. Usually Thoreau turned them down, saying that his walks were important to him and he had "no walks to throw away on company." Sometimes, however, Ellery Channing or Bronson Alcott or Emerson were accepted as walking companions. Emerson has left a good picture of his friend as he started off on one of his afternoon tramps: "Under his arm he carried an old music-book to press plants; in his pocket his diary and pencil, a spy-glass for birds, microscope, jack-knife and twine. He wore a straw hat, stout shoes, strong gray trousers, to brave scrub oaks and smilax and to climb a tree for a hawk's or squirrel's nest. He waded into the pool for water-plants, and his strong legs were no insignificant part of his armor." Add to this that he "was of short stature, firmly built, of light complexion, with strong, serious blue eyes, and a grave aspect—his face covered in later years with a beard," and you have a good candid photograph of Henry Thoreau.

But most of the time Thoreau walked alone. "By my intimacy with nature," he wrote in his journal, "I find myself withdrawn from man. My interest in the sun and the moon, in the morning and evening, compels me to solitude." Henry Thoreau, as he himself said, was "a mystic, a transcendentalist and a natural philosopher to boot." And instead of the one "diary" Emerson credited him with, he kept two notebooks with him on his walks, so that the two facets of his nature, the poet and the naturalist, could both find expression: "I have a commonplace book for facts and another for poetry," he says, "but I find it difficult always to preserve the vague distinction which I had in mind, for the most interesting and beautiful facts are so much the more poetry and that is their success. They are *translated* from earth to heaven. I see that if my facts were sufficiently vital and significant . . . I should need but one book of poetry to contain them all." In fact, Henry Thoreau's special genius was that he could express things that the pure scientist must leave unexpressed and things that the poet has not the scientific knowledge to write about.

But as Thoreau grew older, the naturalist gained ascendancy over the poet. He himself, with his unflinching honesty, was aware of this inner drift. "I fear that the character of my knowledge is from year to year becoming more distinct and scientific," he observes, "that in exchange for views as wide as heaven's scope, I am being narrowed down to the field of the microscope. I see details, not wholes nor the shadows of the whole. I count some parts, and say, 'I know.' "

A part of this increasing preoccupation with fact and detail was due to the waning of that youthful "ecstasy" that must inevitably come with age. But in Thoreau's case the trend was intensified by the growing influence which Louis Agassiz exerted over him. During the Walden days, Thoreau had begun to collect fish, turtles and other wild life and had sent them to Agassiz through a mutual friend. Newly settled at Harvard, Agassiz, who had a passion for detail, was making the first classification of the fauna of America. At first Thoreau was suspicious of the narrowness of the classifier's approach. When a Boston ornithologist said, "If you held the bird in your hand," Thoreau quickly answered, "But I would rather hold him in my affections." Yet as the years passed, science increasingly suppressed the poet. The meticulous scientific study of nature now engrossed Thoreau, and what had been a glorified hobby became a profession.

By a strange stroke of poetic justice, the work that Thoreau loved so intensely was the immediate cause of his death. One cold December day, while he was on one of his long walks, Thoreau lay for too long on the frozen ground counting the rings on the bark of a felled hickory tree. He caught a severe cold which developed first into "a kind of bronchitis" and then into tuberculosis.

By the beginning of 1862, when he was not yet forty-five years old, it was clear to Thoreau that he was dying. There was still so much he longed to do. "If I were to live, I should have much to report on Natural History," he said wistfully. It was as close as this stoic allowed himself to come to an expression of regret. He had always insisted that life must be lived day by day, that only the present moment counted: "In any weather, at any hour of the day or night, I have been anxious to improve the nick of time, and notch it on my stick too; to stand on the meeting of two eternities, the past and future, which is precisely the present moment; to toe that line."

Now, knowing that he must die, Thoreau still "toed that line." When a pious friend tried to talk to him about a world-to-come, he said, "One world at a time." And when his old aunt asked him if "he had made his peace with God," he answered her with his old, hard-bitten humor, "I have never quarreled with him."

Thoreau worked to the end. The *Atlantic Monthly* had asked him to turn some of his old nature lectures into articles. Writing with fingers that trembled from weakness, and coughing incessantly, he worked to make them as good as possible. He tried to arrange for a new edition of *The Week;* he selected some material on his stay in the Maine woods from his journals and made a book of it. He tried to finish his list of birds and flowers, and put his papers in good order.

On November 3, 1861, he had written the last entry in his journal (the fourteenth volume): "All this is perfectly clear to an observant eye, and yet it could easily pass unnoticed by most. . . ." With that he wrote his own epitaph. But instead of an "observant" eye, he should have written "the eye of genius." For it was Thoreau's genius that enabled him to see what most people fail to notice.

Thoreau died on May 6, 1862. He was buried in Sleepy Hollow cemetery. He never married; he never had children; his work met with little success; he was always poor; he was often lonely. But in spite of everything he had known how to love his life. "However mean your life is, meet it and live," he had written, "do not shun it and call it hard names. It is not so bad as you are. It looks poorest when you are richest. The faultfinder will find faults in paradise. Love your life, poor as it is. You may perchance have some pleasant, glorious hours even in a poor-house."

Thoreau lived most of his life in one small New England village, yet his nature was so rich that he always felt that he had "traveled much." In a sense he had. For, "ye fools, the theme is nothing, the life everything, all that interests the reader is the depth and intensity of the life excited." It is this ability of Thoreau's to live in depth and intensity, coupled with his magnificent mastery of prose writing, which has made a typically New England genius into one of the great names of world literature.

In the case of Henry David Thoreau, what he was was as important as what he wrote about. And it was this personal integrity which Emerson spoke of when, at Thoreau's funeral, in a "tender and broken" voice he bade farewell, for Concord and for himself, to the man who had been his friend for so many years. "Wherever there is knowledge," Emerson said, "wherever there is virtue, wherever there is beauty, he will find a home."

FROM CAPE COD BY HENRY DAVID THOREAU

The brig St. John, from Galway, Ireland, laden with emigrants, was wrecked on Sunday morning; it was now Tuesday morning, and the sea was still breaking violently on the rocks. There were eighteen or twenty of the same large boxes that I have mentioned, lying on a green hillside, a few rods from the water, and surrounded by a crowd. The bodies which had been recovered, twenty-seven or eight in all, had been collected there. Some were rapidly nailing down the lids, others were carting the boxes away, and others were lifting the lids, which were yet loose, and peeping under the cloths, for each body, with such rags as still adhered to it, was covered loosely with a white sheet. I witnessed no signs of grief, but there was a sober dispatch of business which was affecting. One man was seeking to identify a particular body, and one undertaker or carpenter was calling to another to know in what box a certain child was put. I saw many marble feet and matted heads as the cloths were raised, and one livid, swollen, and mangled body of a drowned girl,—who probably had intended to go out to service in some American family,—to which some rags still adhered, with a string, half concealed by the flesh, about its swollen neck; the coiled-up wreck of a human hulk, gashed by the rocks or fishes, so that the bone and muscle were exposed, but quite bloodless,—merely red and white,—with wide-open and staring eyes, yet lustreless, dead-lights; or like the cabin windows of a stranded vessel, filled with sand. Sometimes there were two or more children, or a parent and child, in the same box, and on the lid would perhaps be written with red chalk, "Bridget such-a-one, and sister's child." The surrounding sward was covered with bits of sails and clothing. I have since heard, from one who lives by this beach, that a woman who had come over before, but had left her infant behind for her sister to bring, came and looked into these boxes, and saw in one—probably the same whose superscription I have quoted—her child in her sister's arms, as if the sister had meant to be found thus; and within three days after, the mother died from the effect of that sight.

We turned from this and walked along the rocky shore. In the first cove were strewn what seemed the fragments of a vessel, in small pieces mixed with sand and seaweed, and great quantities of feathers; but it looked so old and rusty, that I at first took it to be some old wreck which had lain there many years. I even thought of Captain Kidd, and that the feathers were those which sea-fowl had cast there; and perhaps there might be some tradition about it in the neighborhood. I asked a sailor if that was the St. John. He said it was. I asked him where she struck. He pointed to a rock in front of us, a mile from the shore, called the Grampus Rock, and added,—

"You can see a part of her now sticking up; it looks like a small boat."

I saw it. It was thought to be held by the chain-cables and the anchors. I asked if the bodies which I saw were all that were drowned.

"Not a quarter of them," said he.

"Where are the rest?"

"Most of them right underneath that piece you see."

It appeared to us that there was enough rubbish to make the wreck of a large vessel in this cove alone, and that it would take many days to cart it off. It was several feet deep, and here and there was a bonnet or a jacket on it. In the very midst of the crowd about this wreck, there were men with carts busily collecting the seaweed which the storm had cast up, and conveying it beyond the reach of the tide, though they were often obliged to separate fragments of clothing from it, and they might at any moment have found a human body under it. Drown who might, they did not forget that this weed was a valuable manure. This shipwreck had not produced a visible vibration in the fabric of society.

About a mile south we could see, rising above the rocks, the masts of the British brig which the St. John had endeavored to follow, which had slipped her cables, and, by good luck, run into the mouth of Cohasset Harbor. A little further along the shore we saw a man's clothes on a rock; further, a woman's scarf, a gown, a straw bonnet, the brig's caboose, and one of her masts high and dry, broken into several pieces. In another rocky cove, several rods from the water, and behind rocks twenty feet high, lay a part of one side of the vessel, still hanging together. It was, perhaps, forty feet long, by fourteen wide. I was even more surprised at the power of the waves, exhibited on this shattered fragment, than I had been at the sight of the smaller fragments before. The largest timbers and iron braces were broken superfluously, and I saw that no material could withstand the power of the waves; that iron must go to pieces in such a case, and an iron vessel would be cracked up like an egg-shell on the rocks. Some of these timbers, however, were so rotten that I could almost thrust my umbrella through them. They told us that some were saved on this piece, and also showed where the sea had heaved it into this cove which was now dry. When I saw where it had come in, and in what condition, I wondered that any had been saved on it. A little further on a crowd of men was collected around the mate of the St. John, who was telling his story. He was a slim-looking youth, who spoke of the captain as the master, and seemed a little excited. He was saying that when they jumped into the boat, she filled, and, the vessel lurching, the weight of the water in the boat caused the painter to break, and so they were separated. Whereat one man came away, saying,—

"Well, I don't see but he tells a straight story enough. You see, the weight of the water in the boat broke the painter. A boat full of water is very heavy,"—and so on, in a loud and impertinently earnest tone, as if he had a bet depending on it, but had no humane interest in the matter.

Another, a large man, stood near by upon a rock, gazing into the sea, and chewing large quids of tobacco, as if that habit were forever confirmed with him.

"Come," says another to his companion, "let's be off. We've seen the whole of it. It's no use to stay to the funeral."

Further, we saw one standing upon a rock, who, we were told, was one that was saved. He was a sober-looking man, dressed in a jacket and gray pantaloons, with his hands in the pockets. I asked him a few questions, which he answered; but he seemed unwilling to talk about it, and soon walked away. By his side stood one of the life-boat men, in an oilcloth jacket, who told us how they went to the relief of the British brig, thinking that the boat of the St. John, which they passed on the way, held all her crew,—for the waves prevented their seeing those who were on the vessel, though they might have saved some had they known there were any there. A little further was the flag of the St. John spread on a rock to dry, and held down by stones at the corners. This frail, but essential and significant portion of the vessel, which had so long been the sport of the winds, was sure to reach the shore. There were one or two houses visible from these rocks, in which were some of the survivors recovering from the shock which their bodies and minds had sustained. One was not expected to live.

We kept on down the shore as far as a promontory called Whitehead, that we might see more of the Cohasset Rocks. In a little cove, within half a mile, there were an old man and his son collecting, with their team, the seaweed which that fatal storm had cast up, as serenely employed as if there had never been a wreck in the world, though they were within sight of the Grampus Rock, on which the St. John had struck. The old man had heard that there was a wreck and knew most of the particulars, but he said that he had not been up there since it happened. It was the wrecked weed that concerned him most, rock-weed, kelp, and seaweed, as he named them, which he carted to his barnyard; and those bodies were to him but other weeds which the tide cast up, but which were of no use to him. We afterwards came to the life-boat in its harbor, waiting for another emergency,—and in the afternoon we saw the funeral procession at a distance, at the head of which walked the captain with the other survivors.

On the whole, it was not so impressive a scene as I might have expected. If I had found one body cast upon the beach in some lonely place, it would have affected me more. I sympathized rather with the winds and waves, as if to toss and mangle these poor human bodies was the order of the day. If this was the law of Nature, why waste any time in awe or pity? If the last day were come, we should not think so much about the separation of friends or the blighted prospects of individuals. I saw that corpses might be multiplied, as on the field of battle, till they no longer affected us in any degree, as exceptions to the common lot of humanity. Take all the graveyards together, they are always the majority. It is the individual and private that demands our sympathy. A man can attend but one funeral in the course of his life, can behold but one corpse. Yet I saw that the inhabitants of the shore would be not a little affected by this event. They would watch there many days and nights for the sea to give up its dead, and their imaginations and sympathies would supply the place of mourners far away, who as yet knew not of the wreck. Many days after this, something white was seen floating on the water by one who was sauntering on the beach. It was approached in a boat, and found to be the body of a woman, which had risen in an upright position, whose white cap was blown back with the wind. I saw that the beauty of the shore itself was wrecked for many a lonely walker there, until he could perceive, at last, how its beauty was enhanced by wrecks like this, and it acquired thus a rarer and sublimer beauty still.

Why care for these dead bodies? They really have no friends but the worms or fishes. Their owners were coming to the New

World, as Columbus and the Pilgrims did,—they were within a mile of its shores; but, before they could reach it, they emigrated to a newer world than ever Columbus dreamed of, yet one of whose existence we believe that there is far more universal and convincing evidence—though it has not yet been discovered by science—than Columbus had of this: not merely mariners' tales and some paltry drift-wood and seawood, but a continual drift and instinct to all our shores. I saw their empty hulks that came to land; but they themselves, meanwhile, were cast upon some shore yet further west, toward which we are all tending, and which we shall reach at last, it may be through storm and darkness, as they did. No doubt, we have reason to thank God that they have not been "shipwrecked into life again." The mariner who makes the safest port in Heaven, perchance, seems to his friends on earth to be shipwrecked, for they deem Boston Harbor the better place; though perhaps invisible to them, a skillful pilot comes to meet him, and the fairest and balmiest gales blow off that coast, his good ship makes the land in halcyon days, and he kisses the shore in rapture there, while his old hulk tosses in the surf here. It is hard to part with one's body, but, no doubt, it is easy enough to do without it when once it is gone. All their plans and hopes burst like a bubble! Infants by the score dashed on the rocks by the enraged Atlantic Ocean! No, no! If the St. John did not make her port here, she has been telegraphed there. The strongest wind cannot stagger a Spirit; it is a Spirit's breath. A just man's purpose cannot be split on any Grampus or material rock, but itself will split rocks till it succeeds.

III GUSTAVE FLAUBERT

1821-1880

ONLY TWO YEARS before he died, Gustave Flaubert, a great French writer, gave this advice to his young friend and disciple, Guy de Maupassant: "For an artist there is only one principle: sacrifice everything to Art. Life must be considered by the artist as a means, nothing more, and the first person he should not give a hang about is himself."

Flaubert was one man who practiced what he preached. With an almost religious dedication and a self-restraint that was heroic, he sacrificed his life to his art. "I uprooted the man with both my hands, two hands full of strength and pride," he wrote a friend. "I wished to make of a tree of verdant foliage a bare column to place on its summit as on an altar, I know not what divine flame."

Today the divine flame still burns brightly on the altar; the fame of Gustave Flaubert is world-wide. A realist, a dreamer and an acknowledged master of style, his books have a universal appeal. But what about the living tree that was pruned without mercy until it became the bare column? What about the life of the man, Gustave Flaubert?

Flaubert was born at Rouen where his father, a surgeon, was head of the municipal hospital. A handsome, yellow-haired, blue-eyed boy, Gustave was high-spirited, sensitive and in love with life. But his sensitivity was extreme: "Your friend is a man of wax," he wrote George Sand many years later. "Everything is imprinted on him, penetrates him."

This excess of sensitivity, which gave Flaubert, the writer, the power to live in his characters and to endow them with a reality more persuasive than flesh and blood, forced Flaubert, the man, to retreat from life. Although he needed friendship and affection as much as any man, Flaubert locked himself away from the world and lived like a prisoner in his home at Croisset. "If I go to your house," he explained to George Sand, "I shall have a month of dreaming about my trip. Real pictures will replace in my brain the fictitious pictures which I compose with great difficulty. All my house of cards will topple over."

Flaubert was a born writer. By the time he was eight years old he was already the author of numerous plays which he, his sister Caroline and their friends performed on the family billiard table. "I told you I write some plays," he wrote his school friend, Ernest Chevalier. He continues, "I'll write some novels that I have in mind; they are the beautiful Andalusian, the masked ball, Cardenio, Dorothy, The Moorish woman, the impertinent eavesdropper, the prudent husband." Gustave's use of capital letters may have been uncertain, but his enthusiasm was not. A year later he had become a prolific writer. "We've been busy again on the billiard table," he reports to Ernest. "I have about thirty plays, and there are many which Caroline and I act together. I am writing a poem called A Mother which is as good as The Death of Louis XVI. I am also doing several plays, among others one called The Ignorant Antiquary which makes fun of stupid antiquaries and another which is called Preparations to Receive the King, a farce."

In his youth Flaubert's talent bubbled up exuberantly. "I had a great confidence in myself," he says, "splendid leaps of the soul, something impetuous in my whole personality. My heart was as wide as the world, and I breathed all the winds of heaven." It was only when style had become a fetish with him that the torrent of his invention was restrained and channeled until it became a slow agony for Flaubert to write his books. "You don't know what it is to stay a whole day with your head in your hands trying to squeeze your unfortunate brain so as to find a word," the mature artist wrote to George Sand. "Hard labor at Art is necessary to me before obtaining a water-fall."

Like other French boys of his age and position, Flaubert was sent to boarding school. In those days, schools were stern and rigid, with a discipline that was almost military in its severity. Flaubert, with his high-spirited and romantic nature, hated school, but the friends he made became friends for life. Together with Alfred Le Poittevin, the uncle of Guy de Maupassant, Louis Bouilhet, the poet, and other kindred spirits, the young Flaubert talked passionately of books and ideas and dreamed of the plays and novels he planned to write one day.

Dr. Flaubert, however, had other plans for his son. In those days writing was not considered to be a respectable profession. Dr. Flaubert decided that his son should study law, but Gustave did not give in at once. After graduating from school he stayed at home for a year and wrote two romantic novels. It was only when he himself decided that these were not good enough to be published that he agreed to accept his father's choice of career. Very reluctantly, in 1843, he set out for Paris and the study of law.

From a fellow student, Maxime Du Camp, we have a picture of Gustave Flaubert as he was at this time. "One day in March 1843, while Le Marie [a former college friend of Flaubert's at Rouen] was hammering out Beethoven's funeral march on the piano, and I was slinging rhymes, we heard a peal of the bell, violent, imperious, the ring of a master. I saw a tall fellow come in, with a long, fair beard, and his hat over his ear. Gustave Flaubert was then twenty-one years old. He was of heroic beauty. With his white skin slightly flushed upon the cheeks, his long, fine floating hair, his tall, broad-shouldered figure, his abundant golden beard, his enormous eyes—the color of the green of the sea—veiled under black eyelashes, with his voice as sonorous as the blast of a trumpet, his exaggerated gestures and resounding laugh; he was like those young Gallic chiefs who fought against the Roman armies."

But in spite of his gay manner and his resounding laughter, Flaubert was at this time in a state of despair. It was not just that he was bored with his law books and thought the life of a practicing lawyer both trivial and material; he hated the study of law because it interfered with his dream of becoming a writer.

In a letter to one of his old teachers, he explains his position, "I am as you know, studying law, that is I have bought my law books. I'll start studying in a little while, and expect to pass my entrance examinations in July. I continue to busy myself with Greek and Latin, and shall perhaps busy myself with them always. I love the flavor of those beautiful languages; Tacitus is to me like bronze bas reliefs and Homer is beautiful as the Mediterranean: the same pure, blue waters; the same sun and the same horizon. But what keeps coming back to me every minute, what makes me drop my pen as I take notes, and obliterates my textbooks as I read, is my old love, the same fixed idea: writing! That is why I do not accomplish much, even though I rise very early and go out less than ever.

"I have arrived at a decisive moment: I must go forwards or backwards. It is a question of life and death. When I decide, nothing will stop me, even though I be booed and jeered at by everyone.

You are sufficiently acquainted with my stubbornness and stoicism to believe me. I will pass my bar examinations, but I scarcely think I shall ever plead in court about a party wall or on behalf of some poor father of a family cheated by a wealthy climber. When people speak to me of the bar, saying, 'This young man will make a fine trial lawyer, he's such a fine figure of a man, his voice is so booming,' I confess that my stomach turns and I don't feel myself made for such a completely material, trivial life. . . . This then is what I have resolved: I have in mind three novels, each of them different, each requiring a particular kind of writing. This is enough to prove to myself whether I have talent or not.

"Into them I'll put everything I have—all the style, all the intelligence—and then we'll see."

These were brave words, and intelligent ones. But as an older and wiser Flaubert was to write years later, "One does not make one's destiny, one submits to it." And shortly after Flaubert had made his careful plans, destiny changed them.

In August, Flaubert failed his examinations, an amazing event for a man with a phenomenal memory and a brilliant mind. And at the end of the year, while he was on a Christmas visit to his family, Flaubert suffered the first attack of a nervous ailment, a seeming epileptic attack, which at intervals was to haunt the rest of his life. At that time medicine was not as advanced as it is today, and the illness was never accurately diagnosed. In the confusion of conflicting opinions, Flaubert's doctor father decided to keep his son at home and to treat him himself. The study of law had to be abandoned.

From then on Gustave was free to follow his vocation. And sick as he was, shattered and shocked by this physical accident which had changed him from a young man of exuberant vitality into a semi-invalid, he yet saw clearly the compensation his illness offered him. "One good thing has come out of my illness," he wrote a friend, "and that is that I am allowed to spend my time as I please—no small thing in life. I can think of nothing in the world I enjoy more than a nice room well heated, with the right books and plenty of leisure." By leisure Flaubert meant, of course, time to think and to write.

But at this time Flaubert had not yet succeeded in transforming the "tree of verdant foliage" into a "bare column." He was lonely and he longed for his friends. "When shall we all meet again in Paris," he wrote Louis de Comenin, one of the Paris circle, "in good health and good temper? And yet what a fine thing it would be, a little club of good fellows, all sons of art, living together and meeting once or twice a week to eat a good mouthful, washed down with a good wine and savoring some succulent poet! I love above everything the nervous, substantial, clear phrase with swelling muscle, gleaming skin; I like masculine, not feminine phrases . . . in a little time when I am better, I shall take up my Homer and Shakespeare again. Homer and Shakespeare!—everything is there! the other poets, even the greatest, seem small beside them."

Doctor Flaubert had bought a pleasant country home on the banks of the Seine at Croisset, a village close to Rouen, and Gustave was sent there to convalesce from his illness. The quiet of the countryside, the slow-flowing river, the peaceful garden with its great tulip trees did help him to recover. By the spring of 1845, Gustave was well enough to travel to Italy, where the entire Flaubert family was going in order to keep Caroline and her new husband company on their honeymoon.

But this journey into a wider world did not long distract Flaubert from the inner world that was his natural habitat. From Milan he wrote his friend, Alfred Le Poittevin, who had envied Gustave his Italian journey, "Think, write, work, roll up your sleeves and cut your marble like a good workman who doesn't turn his head and laughs at his task. It is only in the second period of the life of an artist that travel is good; but in the first it is better to express everything that is truly intimate, original, individual with you. Give your muse free rein, ignoring human concerns, and each day you'll feel your mind expanding in a way that will astonish you.

"The only way not to be unhappy is to shut yourself up in Art and to count all the rest as nothing. As for me, I've really been fairly well since resigning myself to be perpetually ill. From now until a day that's far distant I ask for no more than five or six hours in my room, a big fire in the winter and a pair of candles to light at night."

Flaubert was glad when the Italian trip came to an end and he could return to Croisset, to the room with the big fire and the candles at night and the work that was a passion with him. It was a peaceful life but it did not last long. In January, 1846, Dr. Flaubert died, and only three months later the pretty and lively Caroline died too, leaving behind her a newborn baby. Since Caroline's husband was a weak and unreliable man, Flaubert and his mother took the baby to live with them at Croisset. Here, shut away from the world, with the exception of one long journey to the Orient and infrequent business trips to Paris, Flaubert remained until he died, writing and thinking and writing some more, sacrificing all personal living to the writing of the books that were to live in his stead.

In the thirty-four years of life that remained to Flaubert, there was only one serious challenge to this monklike dedication. In the summer of 1846 Flaubert went to Paris in order to commission a sculptor friend, Pradier, to make a bust from Caroline's death mask. At Pradier's studio Flaubert met a blue-eyed, golden-haired young woman in a blue dress. She was a poetess, and her name was Louise Colet. Flaubert fell in love with her and she with him. But six days later, in spite of Louise's tears, Flaubert was back at Croisset. The friendship was to last almost ten years; but in the end, when Louise demanded a bigger share in Flaubert's life than he was willing to give her, she, too, was sacrificed to Art. "Let us seek only tranquility," he wrote her, "let us ask of life only an arm-chair, not a throne; only water to quench our thirst, not drunkenness. Passion is not compatible with the long patience that is a requisite of our calling. Art is vast enough to take complete possession of a man. To divert anything from it is almost a crime; it is a sin against the Idea, a dereliction of duty."

Poor Louise! In spite of her pleading, Flaubert went to see her only at long intervals. But he did like writing letters. After a day of hard work he was glad to sit down and write Louise. For ten years, in spite of quarrels and reproaches, she was his one link with the outside world. He wrote her about his ideas on art, told her what progress his books were making, and, as she, too, was a writer, he gave her good advice on writing: "Work patiently every day an equal number of hours, adopt the habit of a studious and calm life, in the first place you will find a great charm in it, and in the second you will gain strength. I, too, have had the mania for spending nights without sleep, which leads to nothing but exhaustion.

"You should mistrust everything which resembles inspiration, for that is nothing more than a deliberate determination and forced excitement, voluntarily caused, and which did not come of itself; besides we do not live in inspiration; Pegasus walks more often than he gallops, genius consists in showing how to make him take the pace we require, but for that purpose, we must not force his stride, as they say in the riding schools."

Sometimes, however, even the controlled Flaubert gave in to the temptation of letting "Pegasus gallop." "I must love you tonight," he writes Louise in a letter dated 2 A.M., "for I am exhausted. My head feels as though it were being squeezed in an iron vise. Since two o'clock yesterday afternoon (except for about twenty-five minutes for dinner), I have been writing *Bovary*. I am in the midst of love-making. This has been one of the rare days of my life passed completely in illusion from beginning to end. At six o'clock this evening as I was writing the word 'hysterics,' I was so swept away, was bellowing so loudly and feeling so deeply what my little Bovary was going through, that I was having hysterics myself.

"I got up from the table and opened the window to calm myself. My head was spinning. Will what I write be good? I have no idea. No matter; it is a delicious thing to write, whether well or badly—to be no longer yourself but to move in an entire universe of your own creating. To-day for instance, man and woman, lover and beloved, I rode in a forest on an autumn afternoon under the yellow leaves, and I was also the horse, the leaves, the wind, the words my people spoke, even the red sun that made them half-shut their love-drowned eyes."

In spite of Flaubert's renunciation of the world, he felt he was living a rich life. According to his theory of art, the artist must have no life of his own but must live only in his characters. "You can depict wine, love, women and great exploits on the condition that you are not a drunkard, a lover, a husband, or a hero," he wrote. "If you are involved in life, you see it badly; your sight is affected either by suffering or by enjoyment. The artist, in my way of thinking, is a monstrosity, something outside nature." And again: "Passion does not make poetry, and the more personal you are, the weaker. *The less you feel a thing, the fitter you are to express it as it is* (as it *always* is, in itself, in its essence, freed of all ephemeral contingencies). But you must have the capacity to *make yourself feel it.* This capacity is what we call genius: the ability to see, to have your model constantly posing in front of you."

Flaubert had that capacity: he was a genius. But Louise, who had only talent, could not renounce the man she loved and live in her poetry. She demanded more and more of his attention. Finally

Flaubert saw that he would have to choose between Louise and the solitude he needed to write his books. He chose his books. In 1856 the friendship came to an end. From then on Flaubert's whole life was in his writing; his whole world was centered around that life.

From Flaubert's niece we get a picture of that world. "The habits of the house were subordinated to my uncle's tastes. My grandmother having, so to say, no personal life, she lived in the happiness of her family. Her aim was to envelop her son in an atmosphere of perfect calm. In the morning it was forbidden to make the smallest noise; towards ten o'clock there was a violent ring; my uncle's room was entered, and then for the first time everyone seemed to wake. The servant brought the letters and papers, put on the table at the bedside a big glass of water, very cold, and a pipe ready filled; he then drew the curtains, and the light poured in. My uncle took up his letters, looked at the address, but rarely opened any of them before having taken several puffs from his pipe, then still reading, he tapped at the partition to call his mother, who immediately ran in to sit by his bed till he got up.

"He dressed slowly, sometimes stopping to go and read over again some passage in his compositions that interested him. Though far from complicated his dress was never careless, and his ideas of cleanliness were fastidious.

"At eleven o'clock he came down to lunch, where my grandmother, Uncle Parain, the governess and myself were already assembled. At this time my uncle ate little especially in the morning, believing that a full diet produces dullness and indisposition to work; hardly ever any meat; eggs, vegetables, a piece of cheese or fruit, and a cup of cold chocolate. At dessert he used to light his pipe, a little clay pipe, get up and go into the garden, whither we followed him. His favorite walk was the terrace under the rocks, shaded on one side by the old lime trees cut straight like a great wall. It led to the summerhouse in the style of Louis XV, whose windows looked upon the Seine. We rarely went to the summerhouse after lunch.

"Avoiding the midday sun, we used to climb to a spot called 'The Mercury', because of a statue of that god, by which it was once ornamented. It was a second avenue situated above the terrace, and to which a charming path led, deeply shaded; old yew trees in strange shapes grew from the rocks, showing their bare roots, and their ruinous trunks. Quite at the top of the path on a sort of circular space, a bench was hidden under chestnut trees. Through their branches the quiet water was seen, from time to time a cloud rapidly disappearing. It was the smoke of a steamboat. Towards one o'clock a shrill whistle was heard; it was the 'steamer' as the country folks say.

"The signal for departure had been given.

" 'Come', my uncle would say, 'come to lessons, my Caro', and he taking me by the hand, we would both go into his large study, where the outer blinds, carefully kept closed, had not allowed the heat to penetrate; it was nice there, one breathed a scent of oriental beads mixed with that of tobacco and a trace of perfumes coming through the open door of the dressing-room.

"My uncle would put his pipe away on the chimney-piece, select another, fill it, light it, then seat himself on a green leather armchair at the other end of the room; he used to cross one leg over the other, lean back, take a file, and polish his nails. 'Well, what do you remember from yesterday?' I would begin, then naturally get confused, or perhaps I had forgotten. 'I will tell it to you again.' I drew near him, and seated in front of him on a low chair, or on the divan, I used to listen with palpitating interest to the stories, which he made so amusing for me.

"Often in the summer evenings we used to sit all together on the balcony; and remained there for hours, hearing him talk; the nights would come on little by little, the last passers-by had disappeared; on the towing path opposite, the outline of a horse would be faintly seen, drawing a barge, which glided on noiselessly; a light mist spread over the river, two or three boats put off from the shore. Then my uncle would say, 'It is time to return to the Bovary.' "

Flaubert's closest friend was Louis Bouilhet. Bouilhet and Flaubert had known each other during their Rouen schooldays, and Bouilhet had been a medical student of Doctor Flaubert's. But it was not until he gave up medicine to devote himself to the writing of poetry that he and Flaubert became intimate friends. Finding that he could not earn a living by poetry, Bouilhet had taken a job in a Rouen tutoring school, and every weekend he went to Croisset where he and Flaubert talked of books and writing and criticized each other's manuscripts.

In the fall of 1849, Flaubert, having just completed the first draft of a romantic work called *The Temptation of Saint Anthony,* asked Bouilhet and another friend, Maxime Du Camp to come to Croisset for a reading. "If you do not utter howls of enthusiasm," Flaubert shouted as soon as his friends crossed the threshold, "the reason is that nothing is capable of moving you." At the end of the reading, which lasted for four days, eight hours a day, both Bouilhet and Du Camp condemned *The Temptation of Saint Anthony;* they thought the book too romantic, too lyrical and too diffuse. Flaubert was tremendously disappointed but he accepted the verdict of his friends.

Feeling that Flaubert needed a prosaic, everyday type of story that would curb his romantic outbursts, Bouilhet suggested to Gustave that he write about a Dr. Delaunay both of them had known, a former pupil of Doctor Flaubert's who had become a country doctor and whose life had been ruined by a romantic, sentimental, vain and extravagant wife. This was the germ of the novel *Madame Bovary*. It took Flaubert four years of hard, grueling work to write the story. "The entire value of my book, if it has any, will consist of my having known how to walk straight on a hair," he wrote at this time, "balanced above the two abysses of lyricism and vulgarity (which I seek to fuse in analytical narrative). When I think of what it can be I am dazzled. But then, when I reflect that so much beauty has been entrusted to me, I am so terrified that I am seized with cramps and long to rush off and hide—anywhere. I have been working like a mule for fifteen long years. All my life I have lived with a maniacal stubbornness, keeping all my other passions locked up in cages and visiting them only now and then for diversion. Oh, if ever I produce a good book, I'll have worked for it."

The combination of genius, hard work and an almost fanatical artistic integrity paid off in the end: *Madame Bovary* is recognized as one of the great novels of all time. In an era when romanticism and sentimentalism were the style, Flaubert's realistic book blazed a new trail. By the precision of his expression and the accuracy of his observation, he laid bare the essence of truth that underlies even the most commonplace life. He raised the particular story of *Madame Bovary* to the level of the universal: Emma Bovary became every woman.

The novel met with a stormy reception. It appeared first in installments in the *Revue de Paris,* a magazine in which Maxime Du Camp owned a part interest. At the time the *Revue* had incurred the displeasure of the censor because of its "liberalism." As certain of the passages in *Madame Bovary* were written with a frankness that was unusual in those days of literary prudery, the censors used the novel as a pretext for attacking the magazine in which it appeared. Together with the owners of the *Revue,* Flaubert was hauled into court and charged with an "outrage against morals and religion." After a long trial, the judge handed down a verdict of "not guilty," but the decision was accompanied by a moral disapprobation of *Madame Bovary*.

The whole affair disgusted and disheartened the sensitive Flaubert. He had worked on the novel for four years; into it he had put everything he knew as an artist, and to it he had sacrificed his personal life. He believed the novel to be scrupulously honest and therefore worthy of respect. The notoriety and the scandal that had greeted the novel when it appeared in the *Revue* made him more determined than ever to stay shut away from the world, at Croisset.

Madame Bovary appeared in book form in 1857 and was a great success, some of which was undeniably due to the notoriety that had preceded its publication. "I have received very flattering compliments from all my fellow-writers and my book is going to sell unusually well for a first novel," he wrote a friend. "But my ultimate feeling about the trial is one of displeasure. It has caused my book's success to be of a distorted kind, and I do not enjoy having Art mixed up with this kind of thing. I should like to return, once and for all, to the solitude and the silence from which I emerged; I should like to publish nothing, and never again have myself talked about."

In spite of these threats, Flaubert went ahead with his writing. It would have been easier for him to stop breathing than to give up the work that was more important to him than life itself. But this life became lonelier and more and more ingrown. Now even his family saw him only on Sundays.

"I pass entire weeks without exchanging a word with a human being," he wrote George Sand, with whom he had formed an affectionate friendship which once again was almost entirely confined to the writing of letters. "At the end of the week it is not possible for me to recall a single day nor any event whatsoever. I see my mother and my niece on Sundays and that is all. My only company consists of a band of rats in the garret, which makes an infernal racket above my head, when the water does not roar or the wind blow. The nights are black as ink, and a silence surrounds me comparable to that of the desert. Sensitiveness is increased immeasurably in such a setting. I have palpitations of the heart for nothing."

Flaubert's adult life had always been lonely but until now it had not been actively unhappy. But with the outbreak of the Franco-Prussian war Flaubert suffered agonies over what he called "the hopeless barbarism of humanity."

"I don't think there is in France a sadder man than I am!" he wrote George Sand. "What distresses me is 1) the ferocity of men; 2) the conviction that we are going to enter upon a stupid era."

The Germans invaded France, and Croisset was occupied; and now Flaubert suffered, not only for mankind in general, but for Gustave Flaubert in particular. "I'm stifling in gall! These officers who break mirrors with white gloves on, who know Sanskrit and who fling themselves on the champagne, who steal your watch and then send you their visiting card, these civilised savages give me more horror than cannibals."

Under the pressure of his melancholy, the old malady returned. Flaubert suffered a physical and nervous breakdown. In 1873, in the midst of this crisis, the mother who had been home and family and devoted friend for him, died. One by one he lost touch with his friends. The niece he had loved like a daughter married and went away; her husband suffered financial reverses in which Flaubert, who tried to help them, also became involved.

Alone, sick, melancholy, harassed by financial worries, Flaubert never faltered in his devotion to his art. "I am sad no longer," he wrote George Sand. "Yesterday I took up my Saint Antoine—I had to. The Greeks in the time of Pericles devoted themselves to Art without knowing where their next day's bread would come from. Let us be Greek!"

But sometimes the human being in Flaubert still rose up against the artist, and a cry from the heart escaped him. "Everything around me has disappeared," he wrote George Sand, "and now I find I am in a desert." What consolation he could find came to him from another, an even greater fellow-artist. "I am not reading at all, except Shakespeare, whom I am going through from beginning to end. That tones you up and puts new air in your lungs, just as if you were on a high mountain."

Having filled his lungs with mountain air, he returned to his desk. And the books that were to make Flaubert one of the giants of French literature were written. A new and mature version of *The Temptation of Saint Anthony* was published in 1874; *Three Tales,* those perfect and searching masterpieces of the short story, in 1877; and *Bouvard and Pécuchet,* a great satire on the futility of human knowledge and the mediocrity of the human race, and the work thought by many critics to be Flaubert's best, was published after its author's death.

To the end of his life Flaubert never stopped trying to clarify his theories on writing. "I have always tried to go into the soul of things and to stick to the greatest generalities," he wrote George Sand, "and I have purposely turned aside from the accidental and the dramatic. No monsters and no heroes!" And again, "I believe that the rounding of the phrase is nothing. But that *writing well* is everything, because 'writing well is at the same time perceiving well and saying well' (Buffon). The last term is then dependent on the other two, since one has to feel strongly, so as to think, so as to express."

But by "feeling strongly," Flaubert did not mean that an artist should allow his own personality to autograph his work. And when

George Sand, whose own writing was frequently little more than a vehicle for her own ideas, accused Flaubert of suffering from a "lack of convictions," he denied the accusation indignantly. "I am only too full of convictions. But my ideal of Art demands that the artist show none of this, and that he appear in his work no more than God in nature. The man is nothing, the work is everything!"

Flaubert died suddenly on the 8th of May, 1880, of apoplexy. He was alone at Croisset. His last book *Bouvard and Pécuchet* was not quite finished. With a fanatical attention to detail he had read and annotated fifteen hundred books in order to document this novel. The drive and energy that were needed to produce this work of art had undermined the health of the artist. But "the man is nothing, the work is everything!"

From A SIMPLE HEART by Gustave Flaubert

[In the town of Pont-l'Évêque in France, there lived a widow called Madame Aubain whose servant, Félicité, was the envy of everyone in town.

For four pounds a year, Félicité cooked for Madame Aubain and her two children, Paul and Virginie, did their sewing, washing and ironing, bridled their horse, fattened their chickens, and churned their butter. "Her face was thin and her voice sharp. At twenty-five she looked like forty. From fifty onwards she seemed of no particular age; and with her silence, straight figure, and precise movements she was like a woman made of wood, and going by clockwork." Félicité had no life of her own. Faithful and devoted, she was dedicated, body and soul, to her mistress and the children.

In the summertime, whenever the weather was fine, Félicité

would drive out with the Aubains to their farm in the country. On one of these picnics they were chased by a bull. While Madame Aubain and her children ran for safety, Félicité, who had been brought up in the country, bravely held the bull at bay by throwing clods of earth in his face. She was nearly gored by the enraged animal but just managed to save herself by slipping between two rails of a fence. The whole of Pont-l'Évêque talked of this exploit for years. But Félicité did not even suspect that she had done anything out of the ordinary.

When they grew older, Paul and Virginie were sent to boarding school. Félicité missed the children so much she could not sleep and was, in her own words, "destroyed." In her loneliness she asked Madame Aubain to allow her to invite her nephew, Victor, to come and visit her. Madame Aubain granted the necessary permission and, for a time, Victor took lunch with his aunt every Sunday. Then Victor, too, grew up and went to sea as a cabin boy. Each time, when he returned from a voyage, he brought his aunt a present—a box of shells, a coffee cup and, once, a large gingerbread man. Finally Victor sailed off to Havana and never came back. He died of yellow fever.

Félicité was heartbroken. And while she was still mourning for her nephew, fate dealt her an even more terrible blow. Virginie, always a delicate child, contracted pneumonia and died before Madame Aubain and Félicité could reach her in her convent school. The faithful Félicité laid out the dead child, sat up with her for two nights, and followed her coffin to the cemetery on foot.

Madame Aubain and Félicité lived on together at Pont-l'Évêque, lonely and sad. Nothing now interrupted the monotony of their lives but Paul's letters. Unfortunately, however, the news from Paul was disquieting; gay and irresponsible, he was "swallowed up in tavern life and could follow no career."

The years slipped away. People died and new ones came to take their place. Among the new arrivals was a Baron de Larsonnière who brought with him a wife, a sister-in-law, three young ladies, a Negro servant and a parrot. The de Larsonnières became quite friendly with Madame Aubain and when they moved away from Pont-l'Évêque, a few years later, they left the parrot to their friend as "a mark of regard."]

His name was Loulou. His body was green and the tips of his wings rose-pink; his forehead was blue and his throat golden.

But he had the tiresome habits of biting his perch, tearing out his feathers, sprinkling his dirt about, and spattering the water of his tub. He annoyed Madame Aubain and she gave him to Félicité for good.

She endeavored to train him; soon he could repeat "Nice boy! Your servant, sir! Good morning, Marie!" He was placed by the side of the door. . . .

Loulou had been slapped by the butcher-boy for making so free as to plunge his head into his basket; and since then he was always trying to nip him through his shirt. Fabu (as the butcher-boy was called) threatened to wring his neck, although he was not cruel, for all his tattooed arms and large whiskers. Félicité, who was alarmed by such proceedings, put the bird in the kitchen. His little chain was taken off and he roamed about the house.

His way of going downstairs was to lean on each step with the curve of his beak, raise the right foot and then the left; and Félicité was afraid that these gymnastics brought on fits of giddiness. He fell ill and could not talk or eat any longer. There was a growth on his tongue, such as fowls have sometimes. She cured him by tearing the pellicle off with her finger-nails. Mr. Paul was thoughtless enough one day to blow some cigar-smoke into his nostrils, and another time when Mme. Lormeau was teasing him with the end of her umbrella he snapped at the ferrule. Finally he got lost.

Félicité had put him on the grass to refresh him, and gone away for a minute, and when she came back—no sign of the parrot! She began by looking for him in the shrubs, by the waterside, and over the roofs, without listening to the mistress's cries of "Take care, do! You are out of your wits!" Then she investigated all the gardens of Pont-l'Évêque, and stopped the passers-by. "You don't ever happen to have seen my parrot, by any chance, do you?" And she gave a description of the parrot to those who did not know him. Suddenly, behind the mills at the foot of the hill, she thought she could make out something green that fluttered. But on the top of the hill there was nothing. A hawker assured her that he had come across the parrot just before, at Saint-Melaine, in Mère Simon's shop. She rushed there; they had no idea of what she meant. At last she came home with her slippers in shreds and despair in her soul: and as she was sitting in the middle of the garden-seat at Madame's side, telling the whole story of her efforts, a light weight dropped on to her shoulder—it was Loulou! What on earth had he been doing? Taking a walk in the neighborhood, perhaps!

She had some trouble recovering from this, or rather never did recover. As the result of a chill she had an attack of quinsy, and soon afterwards an ear-ache. Three years later she was deaf.

Her little circle of ideas grew still narrower; the peal of church-bells and the lowing of cattle ceased to exist for her. All beings moved as silently as ghosts. One sound only reached her ears now—the parrot's voice.

They carried on conversations, he endlessly repeating the three phrases in his repertory; to which she replied with words that were just as disconnected but uttered what was in her heart. Loulou was almost a son and a lover to her in her isolated state. He climbed up on her fingers, nibbled at her lips and clung to her kerchief; and when she bent her forehead and shook her head gently to and fro, as nurses do, the great wings of her bonnet and the bird's wings quivered together.

When the clouds massed and the thunder rumbled, Loulou broke into cries, perhaps remembering the downpours in his native forests. The streaming rain made him absolutely mad; he fluttered wildly about, dashed up to the ceiling, upset everything, and went out through the window to dabble in the garden; but he was back quickly to perch on one of the firedogs and hopped about to dry himself, exhibiting his tail and his beak in turn.

One morning in the terrible winter of 1847 she had put him in front of the fireplace because of the cold. She found him dead, in the middle of his cage: head downwards, with his claws in the wires. He had died from congestion, no doubt. But Félicité thought he had been poisoned with parsley, and though there was no proof of any kind, her suspicions inclined to Fabu.

She wept so piteously that her mistress said to her, "Well, then, have him stuffed!"

She asked advice of the chemist, who had always been kind to the parrot. He wrote to Havre, and a person called Fallacher undertook the business.

Fallacher kept the parrot a long time. He was always promising it for the following week. After six months he announced that a packing-case had started, and then nothing more was heard of it. It really seemed as though Loulou was never coming back. "Ah they have stolen him!" Félicité thought.

He arrived at last, and looked superb. There he was, erect upon a branch which screwed into a mahogany socket, with a foot in the air, and his head on one side, biting a nut which the bird-stuffer—with a taste for impressiveness—had gilded.

Félicité shut him up in her room. It was a place to which few people were admitted, and held so many religious objects and miscellaneous things that it looked like a chapel and bazaar in one.

With the aid of a bracket Loulou was established over the chimney, which jutted into the room. Every morning when Félicité woke up she saw him there in the dawning light, and recalled old days and the smallest details of insignificant acts in a deep quietness which knew no pain.

Holding as she did no communication with anyone, Félicité lived as insensibly as if she were walking in her sleep. The Corpus Christie procession roused her to life again. Then she went round begging mats and candlesticks from the neighbors to decorate the altar they put up in the street.

In Church she was always gazing at the Holy Ghost in the window, and observed that there was something of the parrot in him. The likeness was still clearer, she thought, on a crude colour-print representing the baptism of our Lord. With his purple wings and emerald body he was the very image of Loulou.

She bought him, and hung him up so that she could see them both together in one glance. They were linked in her thoughts; and the parrot was consecrated by his association with the Holy Ghost, which became more vivid to her eye and more intelligible. The Father could not have chosen to express Himself through a dove, for such creatures cannot speak; it must have been one of Loulou's ancestors surely. And though Félicté looked at the picture while she said her prayers, she swerved a little from time to time towards the parrot.

[In March, 1853, Madame Aubain died at the age of seventy-two. The devoted Félicité mourned for her mistress. "It seemed contrary to the order of things, impossible and monstrous that Madame should die before her."

Paul, who was now married, came with his wife for a couple of days, chose some furniture for himself, sold the rest, and went away again. Now the old servant was alone in the world.]

Félicité went from floor to floor dazed with sorrow.

The next day there was a notice on the door, and the apothecary shouted in her ear that the house was for sale.

She tottered and was obliged to sit down. What distressed her most of all was to give up her room, so suitable as it was for poor Loulou. She enveloped him with a look of anguish when she was imploring the Holy Ghost, and formed the idolatrous habit of kneeling in front of the parrot to say her prayers. Sometimes the sun shone in at the attic window and caught his glass eye, and a great luminous ray shot out of it and put her in an ecstasy.

She had a pension of fifteen pounds a year which her mistress had left her. The garden gave her a supply of vegetables. As for clothes, she had enough to last her to the end of her days, and she economized in candles by going to bed at dusk.

Years and years passed, and the house was neither let nor sold. Félicité never asked for repairs because she was afraid of being sent away. The boards on the roof rotted; her bolster was wet for a whole winter. After Easter she spat blood.

The Mère Simon called in a doctor. Félicité wanted to know what was the matter with her. But she was too deaf to hear, and the only word that reached her was "pneumonia." It was a word she knew, and she answered softly, "Ah! like Madame," thinking it natural that she should follow her mistress.

The time for the festal shrines was coming near. The first one was always at the bottom of the hill, the second in front of the post-office, and the third towards the middle of the street. There was some rivalry in the matter of this one, and the women of the parish ended by choosing Madame Aubain's courtyard.

The hard breathing and fever increased. Félicité was vexed at doing nothing for the altar. If only she could at least have put something there! Then she thought of the parrot. The neighbors objected that it would not be decent. But the priest gave her permission, which so intensely delighted her that she begged him to accept Loulou, her sole possession, when she died.

From Tuesday to Saturday, the eve of the festival, she coughed more often. By the evening her face had shrivelled, her lips stuck to her gums, and she had vomitings; and at twilight next morning, feeling herself very low, she sent for the priest.

Three kindly women were round her during the extreme unction.

Félicité spoke to shadows of her own from time to time. The women went away, and Mère Simon had breakfast. A little later she took Loulou and brought him close to Félicité with the words:

"Come, now, say goodbye to him!"

Loulou was not a corpse, but the worms devoured him; one of his wings was broken and the tow was coming out of his stomach. But she was blind now; she kissed him on the forehead and kept him close against her cheek. Mère Simon took him back from her to put him on the altar.

Summer scents came up from the meadows; flies buzzed; the sun made the river glitter and heated the slates. Mère Simon came back into the room and fell softly asleep.

She woke at the noise of the bells; people were coming out from vespers. Félicité's delirium subsided. She thought of the procession and saw it as if she had been there.

All the school-children, the church singers, and the firemen walked on the pavement, while in the middle of the road the verger armed with his hallebard and the beadle with a large cross advanced in front. Then came the school-master, with an eye on the boys and the sister, anxious about her little girls; three of the daintiest, with angelic curls, scattered rose-petals in the air; the deacon controlled the band with outstretched arms; and the two censer-bearers turned back at every step towards the Holy Sacrament which was borne by monsieur the curé, wearing his beautiful chasuble, under a canopy of dark-red velvet held up by the four churchwardens. A crowd of people pressed behind, between the white cloths covering the house walls, and they reached the bottom of the hill.

A fusillade shook the windowpanes. It was the postilions saluting the monstrance. Félicité rolled her eyes and said as audibly as she could: "Does he look well?" The parrot was weighing on her mind.

Her agony began. A death rattle that grew more and more convulsed made her sides heave. Bubbles of froth came at the corners of her mouth and her whole body trembled.

The clergy appeared in the courtyard. Mère Simon clambered on to a chair to reach the attic window, and so looked straight upon the shrine. Green garlands hung over the altar, which was decked in a flounce of English lace. In the middle was a small frame with relics in it; there were two orange trees at the corners, and all along stood silver candlesticks and china vases, with sunflowers, lilies, peonies, foxgloves, and tufts of hortensia. There was a silver-gilt sugar basin with a crown of violets. Loulou was hidden under roses, and showed nothing but his blue forehead, like a plaque of lapis lazuli.

The churchwardens, singers and children took their places around three sides of the court. The priest went slowly up the steps and placed his great, radiant golden sun upon the lace. Everyone knelt down. There was a deep silence; and the censers glided to and fro on the full swing of their chains.

An azure vapour rose up into Félicité's room. Her nostrils met it; she inhaled it sensuously, mystically; and then closed her eyes. Her lips smiled. The beats of her heart lessened one by one, vaguer each time and softer, as a fountain sinks, and echo disappears; and when she sighed her last breath she thought she saw an opening in the heavens, and a gigantic parrot hovering above her head.

IV SAMUEL LANGHORNE CLEMENS

1835-1910

WHEN HE WAS already a world-famous man, Samuel Clemens took time out from a busy life to give some advice to a young writer who had sent him a manuscript for criticism. It was advice he himself had followed so consistently all his writing life that it can be said to sum up his literary credo:

"Literature is an *art,* not an inspiration," he wrote. "It is a trade, so to speak, and must be *learned.* And its capital is *experience.* I wish to impress upon you this truth: that at the moment you venture outside your own experience, you are in peril. Whatever you have *lived* you can write & by your hard work and genuine apprenticeship you can learn to write well; but what you have not lived you cannot write, you can only pretend to write it."

To some extent all authors draw on this capital of personal experience in writing their books. But Samuel Clemens was an extreme case. Occasionally, as in *The Prince and the Pauper* and *Joan of Arc,* he entered the realm of fantasy or history; but his greatest books reflect his own life. In writing *The Adventures of Tom Sawyer* and *The Adventures of Huckleberry Finn, Roughing It, Life on the Mississippi* and *The Innocents Abroad,* Clemens drew on his own childhood and his wandering, adventurous youth.

Such a literal transcription of reality in the hands of a lesser talent might have produced only journalism or, at best, folk tales of quality. But because Samuel Clemens was greatly gifted, his characters transcend their local setting to become citizens of the world. Despite their American dress, their American humor and their American vernacular, Huck Finn and Tom Sawyer remain archetypes of youth; everyone meets in these characters his own youth. To explore the particular so deeply that you arrive at the universal demands genius. And this is what Samuel Clemens had—an American genius, vital, fresh, optimistic and salted with a grass-roots humor.

Until Samuel Clemens arrived on the scene, American writers had all been Easterners. Steeped in European thought and European culture, they very naturally wrote in the European tradition. But Clemens spoke with a new voice—the voice of the American West. A man of the frontier, he used the homely, vigorous language of the people around him. His humor was often rough, but it was filled with the contagious belly laughter of a country in the making.

Samuel Clemens, unlike most literary men, was no philosopher. He was a man of action. "I still do the thing commanded of Circumstance and Temperament and reflect afterwards," he wrote in his old age. To others he left the great problems and the cosmic searchings; he himself concentrated on the small world he knew from his own direct experience. And best of all he knew himself: "My life has been constantly devoted to the study of the human race—that is to say the study of myself," he declares, "for in my individual person I am the entire human race compacted together. The shades of differences between other people and me serve to make a variety and prevent monotony, but that is all; broadly speaking we are all alike."

Fundamentally, Samuel Clemens was a descendant of the old

troubadours. He began his career by talking his stories, "spinning yarns" by the hour whenever he could find anyone who would listen. Uninterested in whys and wherefores, he let life flow through him into his books with a minimum of conscious thought. Because of this his life is the best key to his books and his books, in turn, unlock his life.

That life began on November 30, 1835, in a log cabin in a small Missouri village called Florida where his father, John Marshall Clemens, kept a general store. Sam, a delicate baby, was the fourth child, and Florida was the fourth place his parents had lived in since their marriage. John Marshall Clemens and his wife, Jane Lamkin, descendants of Virginia gentlefolk, had not always lived in log-cabin style. But, having lost his fortune in the financial crash of 1834, John Clemens, a proud man, had no desire to live on in poverty in a place where he had once been rich; he could not bear to be pitied by his old friends. So, loading his family and his household possessions onto a wagon, he set out hopefully for what was then the "Far West." By profession John Clemens was a lawyer (everyone called him "Judge" until he died), but there was little demand for legal services in the small towns of the American frontier. To support his family he opened a general store. But he was an austere and idealistic man who had no talent at all for business so that, after only a few years, the Florida store failed.

Once again the family decided to try their luck in a new environment. This time their choice was Hannibal, a town of 1500 inhabitants on the banks of the Mississippi River. Sam, who was only four years old when he arrived in his new home, always remembered it as he first saw it: "a white town drowsing in the sunshine of a summer morning—the great Mississippi, the magnificent Mississippi, rolling its mile-wide tide along—the dense forest on the other side."

Hannibal was a good place for a boy to grow up. The surrounding countryside with its hills and forests was a perfect playground, and the great river was not only fun to swim in, it was a window on a big and colorful world. Whenever a boat steamed up the river, the whole town trooped down to the dock; even the pigs joined the procession, trotting to the wharves in the hopes of getting some garbage from the ships. With their "clean, white railings; the upper decks black with passengers" and the Captain standing "by the big bell, calm and imposing; the envy of all," the river boats were a glamorous sight. All the boys in Hannibal dreamed of becoming captains or steersmen. And although, now and then, like boys everywhere, they shifted their ambitions to becoming pirates or circus people, "these ambitions faded each in turn"; Sam Clemens says, "the ambition to be a steamboat man always remained."

When he was young, Sam was small for his age, with a crest of sand-colored hair and humorous eyes. He was the leader of a band of boon companions who roamed the countryside barefoot from morning to night, played pirates, dug for buried treasure, smoked from the age of nine, rolled boulders down the hillside onto passing wagons, played hooky from the school they hated, and almost drowned time and again in the Mississippi before they finally succeeded in learning how to swim. Sam reported that he himself nearly drowned seven times.

Mrs. Clemens had plenty to worry about. Luckily she was a valiant woman, small in body but large in heart. "A heart so large," her son says, "that everybody's grief and everybody's joys found welcome in it."

From his mother Sam inherited a generous heart and an eager interest in the world and its people. From her, too, came the ability to "say a humorous thing with the perfect air of not knowing it to be humorous," a trick which was to stand him in good stead in later years when he stood on the lecture platform. And from his mother, also, he took the habit of "pulling his words in a drawl."

Because Sam resembled her in so many ways, Mrs. Clemens always understood this son well. Sometimes too well. When he told her his astonishing tales of adventure, she listened with more than the customary "grain of salt."

"You don't believe anything that child says, I hope?" a neighbor asked.

"Oh yes, I know his average," Mrs. Clemens answered, "I discount ninety per cent. The rest is pure gold."

Until he was twelve years old Sam led the easygoing, mischievous, adventurous life that was suited to his years and his temperament. He drew on this colorful life later in writing the adventures of Tom Sawyer and his friend, Huckleberry Finn. He himself served as model for Tom; the son of the town drunkard, Tom Blankenship, was the original from which Huck was drawn. "In Huckleberry Finn, I have drawn Tom Blankenship exactly as he was," Samuel Clemens writes in his autobiography. "He was ignorant, unwashed, insufficiently fed; but he had as good a heart as ever anybody had. . . . He was the only really independent person—boy or man—in the community and by consequence he was tranquilly and continuously happy and was envied by all the rest of us."

But life in Hannibal, Missouri, was not all young adventure. A frontier town and a river town, it was a magnet for lawless people. At an early age the free-roving Sam witnessed sights that most children of his age are spared. At various times, he saw a tramp burn to death, a man shot dead at high noon, a slave "struck down with a chunk of slag for some small offense," and colored men and women being led to market like animals, chained one to the other. Sam had been given a strict religious training, and this, combined with the tender conscience he was to suffer from all his life, led him to look upon these terrible sights as "inventions of Providence to beguile me to a better life. It sounds curious and innocent and conceited now," he says, looking back at his youth from the vantage point of age, "but–it would not have surprised me, nor even overflattered me, if Providence had killed off the whole community in trying to save an asset like me."

This is humorous talk, but, like most true humor, it comes out of a deep awareness of the mixed and confused motives that inspire human lives. "Everything human is pathetic," Sam Clemens said later in life; "The secret source of humor itself is not joy but sorrow."

With the death of John Clemens in 1847, Sam saw sorrow, no longer vicariously, but at first hand. His father's death came at a time when the family fortunes were just beginning to take a turn for the better. The "Judge" had been elected to the clerkship of the surrogate court, a position that commanded a comfortable salary. The Clemenses had been poor ever since they arrived in Hannibal, but in that little frontier town "rich" and "poor" were just words. "Everybody was poor but didn't know it," Clemens writes, "and everybody was comfortable and did know it." But John Clemens's death left his family no longer just "poor"; they were destitute.

The only tangible asset they had was 100,000 acres of Tennessee land which John Clemens had bought for $400 in 1825 when he was living in the state. In 1847 there was still no market for the land, but the thought comforted John Clemens as he lay dying. "Cling to the land," he urged the family gathered around his deathbed, "cling to the land and wait."

From that moment on, the Tennessee land became a family dream. Sam always felt that this unreal hope of future wealth had been an unsettling influence. "It kept us hoping and hoping during forty years and forsook us at last," he says. "It put our energies to sleep and made visionaries of us—we were always going to be rich next year—no occasion to work. It is good to begin life poor; it is good to begin life rich—these are wholesome; but to begin it poor and prospectively rich! The man who has not experienced it cannot imagine the curse of it."

The immediate effect this dream of future wealth had on the Clemens family was to make them feel that since their unfortunate financial situation was not a permanent one, they need only improvise some temporary relief. Instead of planning dependable careers for the boys, they thought only in terms of expedients. Orion, the eldest son, who was a book and job printer living in St. Louis, sent his family in Hannibal three dollars out of his weekly salary of ten dollars; Pamela, Sam's older sister, gave piano lessons; and Sam, just twelve years old, was permitted to leave school and to go as an apprentice to Joseph Ament, the owner of the Hannibal *Courier*. It was Sam himself who was eager to go to work. He had always detested school and was glad to leave it. "I will promise anything," he told his mother, whose one concern was that he should be a "good" boy, "if you just won't make me go to school." According to the agreement made with Ament he was to work for "board and clothes." In practice this turned out, as Sam reported later, "to be more board than clothes and not much of either."

Although he changed jobs half a dozen times, Sam worked long hours for little pay during the ten following years. In his old age he declared that those years, from twelve to twenty-two, were the *only* years he ever worked: "From the time my father died, March 24th, 1847 until the end of 1856, or the first days of 1857 I worked—not diligently, not willingly, but fretfully, lazily, repiningly, complainingly, disgustedly, and always shirking the work when I was not watched When I escaped from the printing office I ceased to be a worker and ceased permanently."

Once in a while during this time, Sam Clemens did some original writing. Once when Orion was away he contributed a few "spicy" items to a paper his brother owned, pieces which had a gossipy success and which made trouble for Orion; and in 1851 he wrote down a few anecdotes and sent them to the *Saturday Evening Post,* which accepted them and printed them anonymously. But in spite of this success Sam Clemens never once during all these years thought seriously of becoming a writer. Whatever ambition he had was for adventure. He longed to travel and he hoped to make use of his trade to become a "tramp printer," earning his way around the world. In fact, he got as far as New York, working his way from job to job. But he hardly thought of this as travel and so he satisfied his craving for adventure by reading about other people's journeys. He was fascinated by a book he read about South America and swore to himself that he, too, would "go to the headwaters of the Amazon and collect cocoa and trade in it and make a fortune." But for a long while the Amazon, like the Tennessee land, remained only a dream.

Then one day luck helped him to get started on a real adventure. He was walking along a Cincinnati street on a windy day when a fifty dollar bill fluttered down from the sky and landed at his feet. After a struggle with his conscience, Sam forced himself to advertise his find in the local paper. When no one claimed the money he took his fifty dollars, added to it a small sum he had saved, and set off for the Amazon. His plan was to take a river boat as far as New Orleans and transfer there to a ship bound for South America. The pilot of the river boat was Horace Bixby, a genial companion and one of the best steersmen on the Mississippi. He took a liking to his exuberant young passenger, allowing him to take the wheel and steer the boat during the daytime. Sam Clemens had dreamed all his childhood of becoming a pilot on the great river that he had known since he was four years old. Now with the wheel of a real steamship between his hands, the old dream woke to new life. Forgetting about the Amazon, he asked Bixby to teach him to become a steersman. Bixby agreed, setting $500 as the price of tuition. When Sam told him that this was more money than he could lay his hands on, Bixby agreed to take $100 on account, the remaining $400 to be paid out of his pupil's future earnings. Sam borrowed the $100 from his sister's husband and embarked happily on what he believed was to be his life's work.

As an apprentice steersman, Sam Clemens not only "learned the river," he also, as he puts it, "became personally and familiarly acquainted with all the different types of human nature that are to be found in fiction, biography, or history." The colorful, exciting river years proved the best possible schoolroom for a man who believed that a writer should never venture "outside his own experience." Out of the sights and sounds and moods of the Mississippi, out of the varied lives and personalities of the people who traveled it, Samuel Clemens was to weave a book of epic caliber, the famous *Life on the Mississippi.*

Sam won his license as a river pilot when he was just twenty-three years old; it was a position that commanded a salary equal, at that time, to that earned by the President of the United States. During these years, Clemens gave no thought to literature, although Horace Bixby says that "Sam was always scribbling." The truth is that he loved his calling. "Piloting on the Mississippi River was not work to me," he writes in his autobiography, "it was play—delightful, vigorous, adventurous play—and I loved it."

He also loved telling stories to his fellow pilots, and whenever his ship docked he was the center of an uproarious group. "Sam

Clemens was much given to spinning yarns so funny that his hearers were convulsed," a colleague of those days reports, "and yet all the time his own face was perfectly sober." This "spinning of yarns" was always at the heart of the Clemens genius. When he became a professional writer he addressed his stories to the ear rather than the eye, writing as he spoke, using the rhythms of ordinary speech rather than the literary prose so fashionable among the other writers of his day. This gave his style the vitality, the simplicity and the permanence which has caused critics to call him the Abraham Lincoln of American literature.

In 1861 the outbreak of the Civil War put an end to traffic on the Mississippi. Sam Clemens was out of a job. But still he did not think of turning his talent for storytelling into a career. More interested in living life than in writing about it, he embarked on a series of adventures. In turn he became a Confederate soldier (a very brief interlude), a pioneer and a gold miner. To his gay and eager spirit, everything was exciting, everything was colorful. Unfortunately, everything failed. At twenty-seven Samuel Clemens was penniless, out of work and completely uncertain of his future. Happy-go-lucky and irresponsible, he just lived gaily from day to day until, once again, luck started him off in a new direction.

During his unsuccessful though colorful mining days, Sam, like a good son, had written long letters to his mother, who was living in Keokuk, Iowa, with his sister, Pamela. The letters were vivid and humorous and, because many people in America at that time were infected with the gold-mining fever, the Keokuk paper decided to publish some of the Clemens letters. Orion, then living in Nevada, was sent clippings by his family and he, in turn, showed his brother's work to a friend on the staff of the Virginia City *Enterprise.* This reporter, in turn, passed them along to Joe Goodman, the editor in chief, a man who recognized talent when he saw it.

He offered Clemens a job on the *Enterprise* at $25.00 a week. Sam would have preferred to continue his mining operations, but he was having no luck. In addition, his debts were mounting. Very reluctantly he accepted the *Enterprise* offer and hiked the 130 miles to Virginia City.

The *Enterprise* was a stimulating influence in the American newspaper world of the day. Staffed by a fearless and brilliant group of men, it offered Samuel Clemens a perfect environment in which to develop his talent. His first contributions, still unsigned, were in the form of letters. Stimulating, timely, and stamped with the original, clear-sighted yet tolerant brand of humor that was to become the Clemens trademark, the letters from the very outset attracted attention. They were reprinted by other newspapers and quoted so widely that even the easygoing, fun-loving Clemens was shrewd enough to see that he had a future waiting for him in the field of newspaper writing.

Realizing that he could not build a reputation on unsigned pieces, he decided to take a pen name, a customary procedure for writers of his day. During his happy river years, Clemens had written down some of his yarns and sent them off to a paper. One of these ventures had sad results. There was a garrulous old pilot, Isaiah Sellers, who loved to contribute long-winded reminiscences to a New Orleans journal under the pseudonym of *Mark Twain,* a call used by Mississippi pilots in taking soundings on the river. Sellers and his pieces were the laughingstock of his colleagues, and Sam Clemens could not resist writing a take-off on the old man. The parody was a very clever one. It amused the other pilots but it humiliated Isaiah Sellers so deeply that he never ventured into print again. Sam had not meant to hurt the old man and his conscience reproached him. Now, as a sort of belated recompense, he decided to take the pen name of his erstwhile victim. In this way Sellers acquired a place in literary history by reflected glory.

The name was short, clear and original, and it caught on at once. From the beginning it stood for a homespun wisdom, a clear-eyed intelligence and a fresh brand of humor. Soon also it was to become a weapon in the crusade that Mark Twain fought all his life against hypocrisy and cruelty of all kinds. For Samuel Clemens was never just a writer of belles-lettres. Beneath the gay face he showed the world, he was a serious man preaching an earnest message. "Humor is only a fragrance, a decoration," he said. "Often it is merely an odd trick of speech and spelling. Humor must not professedly teach and it must not professedly preach, but it must do both. I have always preached. If humor came of its own accord and uninvited I have allowed it a place in my sermon, but I have not written the sermon for the sake of the humor. I should have written the sermon just the same, whether any humor applied for admission or not."

From the *Enterprise,* Mark Twain graduated to the *Morning Call,* a San Francisco paper so small that, as he puts it, he was "*the* reporter," covering all the city news from police courts to theaters. At that time San Francisco was a center for a witty company which included, among others, Bret Harte and Artemus Ward. With his ready humor, his independent spirit, and his talent for generating laughter, Mark Twain was welcomed into the group with enthusiasm. It was to Artemus Ward that he first told his famous story of the jumping frog. Ward was so delighted with the tale that he urged his friend to write it down, even offering to print it in a book of his own sketches that was just then being readied for publication. Twain did not finish the story in time for Ward's book but it appeared later on in a New York paper, the *Saturday Press.* It was a rollicking tale which treated outrageous exaggerations with absolute seriousness. Broadly humorous and saturated with the spirit of the frontier, it created a sensation. "Mark Twain's story in the *Saturday Press* of Nov. 18th., called 'John Smiley and His Jumping Frog,' has set all New York in a roar," a San Francisco paper reported, "and he may be said to have made his mark. It is voted the best thing of the day."

With the "Jumping Frog" the name Mark Twain became known from coast to coast. And with success came new opportunities. A San Francisco newspaper sent him to the Sandwich Islands as its special correspondent, and the letters he sent home from there added fresh laurels to his crown. Returning to San Francisco, he found himself the talk of the town. On the advice of a friend, he decided to exploit this new popularity by giving a series of lectures on his trip. Shy, funny, original and wise in a humorous way, his success on the lecture platform was immediate; and until 1906, lecturing proved to be a profitable side line to the Clemens career.

"In October, 1866, I broke out as a lecturer," Mark Twain comments in his autobiography, "and from that day to this I have always been able to gain my living without doing any work; for the writing of books and magazine matter was always play, not work, I enjoyed it; it was billiards to me."

During this first lecture tour Mark Twain spoke in all the principal towns of California and Nevada until what at first had been a novel and exciting experience turned into a repetitious grind. Monotony was something Sam Clemens was never able to accept. Even as a boy, while leading a life that was satisfying to all the other Hannibal boys, Sam Clemens had shown in his diary that he was bored: "Got up, washed, went to bed," he wrote. Later on, during his adventurous frontier days, he had shown the same impatience of the everyday whenever there was a pause between one adventure and the next: "24th. Rained all day, meals as before.

25th. Same as above." All his life long the "same as above" was not good enough for Samuel Clemens. Life was too rich, too exciting to be wasted in repetition. So now, when lecturing lost the first, fine flavor of novelty, he looked around for fresh adventure. "Laid out a plan to sail westward from San Francisco and go around the world," he reports. The *Daily Alta,* a San Francisco newspaper, was ready and willing to underwrite the new venture, commissioning him to write fifty letters of about 2,000 words each at $20.00 a letter.

In high spirits, Mark Twain set off on his journey. But, stopping off in St. Louis to visit his family, he heard of something that was even more exciting to him. A group of distinguished people had chartered the steamship *Quaker City* to take them on a tour of the Mediterranean and the Holy Land. This venture was something new: it was the first try at group travel, the ancestor of all the cruises of today. Persuading the *Daily Alta* people to pay his passage on the *Quaker City* in addition to commissioning the travel letters, Mark Twain recast his plans and sailed with the party.

The *Quaker City* trip proved to be a turning point in Mark Twain's life in more ways than one. It provided him with material for a travel book which weaned him from journalism and started him off in the field of quality writing. It also brought him the fulfillment of his personal life.

The seventeen tourists who were aboard were a congenial company, and Mark Twain, as a well-known journalist, was one of the star features of the group. "There was a table from which was sure to come a peal of laughter," a fellow passenger reports, "and all eyes are turned towards Mark Twain whose face is perfectly mirth-provoking. Sitting lazily at the table, scarcely genteel in his appearance, there is something I know not what, that interests and attracts. I saw to-day at dinner, venerable divines and sage-looking men convulsed with laughter at his drolleries and quaint, odd manners."

Charley Langdon, of Elmira, New York, a boy of eighteen, had developed a great admiration for the celebrated writer who was his fellow passenger, and every once in a while the good-natured Samuel Clemens would drop in at the boy's cabin for a chat. On one of these visits, Charley showed his friend a miniature of his sister, Olivia, a delicate, sweet-faced girl with a spiritual expression. Mark Twain, the rough, none-too-well-educated product of the frontier and the mining camp, a man of thirty-three, worshiped a Victorian ideal of womanhood, the pure, sweet, noble girl. "Our heroes are men who do things we recognize with regret and sometimes with a secret shame that we cannot do," he was to write many years later. "We find not much in ourselves to admire, we are always privately wanting to be like somebody else. If everybody was satisfied with themselves there would be no heroes." Or heroines. The gentle, refined girl of the miniature, so obviously everything he was not, became a sort of heroine for Mark Twain. He fell in love with her on the spot and swore to himself in the romantic fashion of those sentimental days that one day he would marry Olivia Langdon.

They met in New York, introduced by Charley, the following December. "She was slender and beautiful and girlish," Mark Twain says, "and she was both girl and woman. Under a grave and gentle exterior burned inextinguishable fires of sympathy, energy, devotion, enthusiasm and absolutely limitless affection. She lived upon her spirit whose hopefulness and courage were indestructible."

Olivia, who had been a semi-invalid since suffering a bad fall on the ice at the age of sixteen, was at first somewhat overpowered by the rough, gay, sometimes vulgar man who loved her so tumultuously. But in the end she succumbed to this force of nature that was Samuel Clemens. She called him "Youth" until she died. " 'Youth' was my wife's pet name for me," he writes. "It was gently satirical but also affectionate. I had certain mental and material peculiarities proper to a much younger person than I was." He kept those "peculiarities" until he died. Watching her father run upstairs on his seventieth birthday, his daughter, Clara, said, "Father is younger now than I have ever felt." It was out of this imperishable youth that Mark Twain wrote his epics of boyhood.

Samuel Clemens and Olivia Langdon were married on February 2, 1870. It proved to be an exceptionally happy marriage. Not only was Olivia a loving wife and a devoted mother to her three daughters, she was also from the beginning her famous husband's editor and literary advisor. "In the beginning of our engagement," he says, "the proofs of my first book, *The Innocents Abroad,* began to arrive and she read them with me. She was my faithful, judicious and painstaking editor from that day forth until within three or four months of her death—a stretch of more than a third of a century."

With his personal life resolved to his perfect satisfaction, Mark Twain concentrated on his writing. The letters he had sent home to the *Alta* and the *New York Tribune* from the *Quaker City* had blazed a new trail in travel literature. Until Mark Twain arrived on the writing scene, American travelers had displayed a sort of national inferiority complex. In indiscriminate awe and admiration, they bowed low before everything European and antique, whether it was good, bad or indifferent. Mark Twain had the courage to look at the old world with new and candid eyes.

His travel letters enjoyed such a spectacular success that Elisha Bliss, Jr., of the American Publishing Company of Hartford, asked Mark Twain to make the letters into a book. After some argument with the *Alta* people, who were reluctant to relinquish their copyright, Clemens agreed to do as Bliss asked. It is interesting to note that as soon as he set to work Mark Twain found that the letters he had fought to regain from the *Alta* were of only minor use to him. There was a great difference between what he called "book matter" and "newspaper matter."

"The letters had been written here and there and yonder," he says, "as opportunity had given me a chance working moment or two during the feverish flight around Europe or in the furnace heat of my stateroom aboard the *Quaker City,* therefore they were loosely constructed and needed to have some of the wind and water squeezed out of them. I used several of them—ten or twelve perhaps. I wrote the rest of *The Innocents Abroad* in sixty days and I could have added a fortnight's labor with the pen and gotten along without the letters altogether. I worked every night from eleven or twelve until broad day in the morning, and as I did 200,000 words in the sixty days, the average was more than 3,000 words a day."

The Innocents Abroad was published in August, 1869; it sold 5,170 copies the first month. By the end of the year 31,000 books were in circulation, a record for those days. Poetic in feeling, yet filled with carefully observed facts, *The Innocents Abroad* steered midway between a refusal to admire everything European indiscriminately and a surmise that there was more to be extracted from European culture than a plain American might see at first sight. In a vocabulary that, unlike the rest of the writing of that period, was "made in America," he wrapped his home truths in a dry and witty humor: "They spell it Vinci and pronounce it Vinchy; foreigners always spell better than they pronounce." Or again, "Wagner's music is not as bad as it sounds." Acclaimed by critics and public alike, *The Innocents Abroad* made Mark Twain the most widely read author in America.

Mark Twain now settled down to work. Drawing on the experiences of his adventurous youth he wrote one great book after another. *Roughing It* was distilled out of his pioneering-mining days.

Tom Sawyer and *Huckleberry Finn* broke with tradition and presented boy-heroes who were neither Fauntleroys nor Peck's Bad Boys but masterpieces of true-to-life youth. *Life on the Mississippi* told of the colorful river years with a poetic sweep that has made the book a classic.

With his gay and gregarious nature, Mark Twain's house in Hartford was, during the winter months, a mecca for friends from all over the world. But in the summers he retired with his family, which in time included three daughters, to his sister-in-law's farm near Elmira, New York. Here he could work undisturbed, and the talent which had for so long lain dormant asserted itself at last, pouring out in a torrent of creation which absorbed and satisfied Mark Twain. "Nothing grieves me now; nothing troubles me, nothing bothers me or gets my attention," he wrote his publisher. "I don't think of anything but the book [*Roughing It*] and don't have an hour's unhappiness about anything, and don't care two cents whether school keeps or not."

Every morning right after breakfast Mark Twain retired to his hillside study where he could work completely undisturbed. He remained there until 5 o'clock in the afternoon, not even taking time out for lunch. A prolific writer, he plunged into his work impetuously with only the vaguest conscious idea of what he intended to say. Starting with a few characters or situations, he trusted Providence to direct his pen: "As long as a book could write itself," he says, "I was a faithful and interested amanuensis and my industry did not flag, but the minute the book tried to shift to my head the labor of contriving its situations, I put it away and dropped it out of my mind. . . . The reason was very simple—my tank had run dry; the stock of materials in it was exhausted; the story could not go on without materials. . . ."

In case of a sudden blockage in the flow of his creative output,

Mark Twain always kept two or three unfinished manuscripts going at once, shifting from one to the other as inspiration waxed and waned. "It was by accident that I found out that a book is pretty sure to get tired along about the middle and refuse to go on with its work until its powers and its interests should have been refreshed by a rest and its depleted stock of raw materials reinforced by lapse of time. It was when I reached the middle of Tom Sawyer that I made this invaluable find." When the tank that was fueling this particular book ran dry, he put the manuscript away. It was two years before he looked at it again; then, suddenly, he was able to finish the story: "It was then that I made the great discovery that when the tank runs dry you've only to leave it alone and it will fill up again in time, while you are asleep—also while you are at work at other things and are quite unaware that this unconscious and profitable cerebration is going on."

At fifty, Samuel Clemens's life had reached its high point. He was acknowledged as the greatest writer of his time; he was happily married; he had three daughters whom he loved devotedly; and he had earned for himself a material prosperity that was ample to make life pleasant and gracious for him. "I am frightened at the proportions of my prosperity. It seems to me that whatever I touch turns to gold," he remarked to a friend. But he was not content to rely on his writing to supply him with added gold. Mark Twain loved the world—and the world loved him. He wanted to partake of a rich social diet and at the same time live luxuriously. And, from his earliest childhood when the dream of future riches had first come to him in the guise of the Tennessee land on through the mining days with their adventure and ever-living hope of discovering gold, gambling had been a necessity of life to Samuel Clemens. Now that his existence was peaceful, now that his books were earning as much money as he needed for his daily life, the temptation to invest that money and gamble with it for high stakes was like a call to adventure. There were no silver mines in the East; there were no exciting rivers to navigate; he was a family man now committed to a settled, domestic life. But his adventurous nature still craved excitement and, looking around for an outlet to satisfy this need, he discovered a new field where thrills were still to be found: inventions. And in this department there was no dearth of opportunity. "All through my life I have been the easy prey of the cheap adventurer," he wrote rather bitterly in his old age. "He came, he lied, he robbed and went his way and the next one arrived by the next train and began to scrape up what was left."

Over a period of years, Mark Twain sponsored one wildcat scheme after the other. He invested his money in a patent steam generator, in a new type of steam pulley, a new method of marine telegraphy, and a process of engraving which was to revolutionize illustrating. Between January, 1881, and January, 1882, alone, he sank $100,000 into a variety of inventions, all of which turned out to be duds. The most disastrous of all these get-rich-quick ventures was the Paige typesetter. In ten years that unworkable white elephant drained away more than $190,000 of the money Mark Twain had earned through his writing.

Even an author of his fame and earning power cannot afford that degree of financial loss. Casting about a little desperately now for a fresh source of revenue, Mark Twain hit upon the idea of becoming his own publisher and thus earning for himself not only the author's royalties but the publisher's share of the profits as well. With his niece's husband, Charles L. Webster, serving as manager, he founded the publishing firm of Charles L. Webster & Co. Mark Twain's writings could be counted on to bring in a handsome revenue, and for a time the new firm prospered. It even branched out and published the very remunerative memoirs of General Grant and a life of Pope Leo XIII. But when in 1893 a financial panic hit the country, the firm's inefficient management combined with the generally depressed state of business forced Charles L. Webster & Co. into bankruptcy. In addition, the Paige Typesetter Machine, which for so long had taken the place of the Tennessee land as the family dream, failed to pass its final tests and had to be abandoned.

All over the world newspapers flaunted banner headlines: Mark Twain a bankrupt. In this time of humiliation and trial the greatness of Mark Twain's nature asserted itself. Although he was not legally bound to assume the debts of the firm, he elected to accept full responsibility for them. In those panic-dominated days many businessmen were turning over to their creditors whatever assets they possessed and then retiring from the situation. Mark Twain decided to stand up to his moral obligation: he would go out and earn the money so that all his creditors could be paid 100 cents on each of their dollars.

At the age of fifty-nine, depressed and in uncertain health, he returned to the lecture platform. The size of his debt dictated the scope of his tour. In 1895, accompanied by his loyal wife and his daughter Clara, Mark Twain set off on a lecture trip that was to last a year and that took him around the world.

Aware of the difference between speech and literature, Mark Twain was not content to take the easy way by reading from his books. A "spinner of yarns" at the outset of his career, he composed his lectures, not as he would have written them for the printed page, but as talks to be given to a live audience. "Written things are stiff, inflexible, and will not lend themselves to happy and effective delivery with the tongue—where their purpose is merely to entertain, not instruct," he said. "They have to be limbered up, broken up, colloquialized and turned into the common forms of unpremeditated talk—otherwise they will bore the house and not entertain it."

The lecture tour was an overwhelming success. And aside from the money it earned, it also supplied Mark Twain with material for a new book, *Following the Equator*. By 1898 every creditor had been paid off in full.

All his life long Samuel Clemens had boasted that he was born under a lucky star. "The proverb says, 'born lucky, always lucky,' " he was fond of saying. This faith in his luck sustained him on many an unhappy occasion. But during the last years of his life, his luck seemed to desert him. He was overwhelmed by a series of disasters. His oldest daughter, a brilliant girl, died at twenty-three and his wife died after two years of painful invalidism in 1904. In his youth Mark Twain's buoyant nature had made him supremely confident in the face of life. With sorrow, that confidence left him. Now the excess of optimism, so long an ingredient of the Clemens nature, turned into an excess of pessimism. The only thing that was left him during these last tragic years was work: "I don't mean that I am miserable," he wrote a friend, "no, worse than that—indifferent, indifferent to nearly everything but work. I like that; I enjoy it and stick to it. I do it without purpose and without ambition; merely for the love of it."

Unfortunately, however, the old creative strength that had welled up like a geyser during his optimistic youth and middle years failed with age and sadness. Never a careful worker, Mark Twain had been content to let his writing flow from him in an uninhibited, natural splurge of unthinking creation. The output of such a writer inevitably includes a certain proportion of waste product. "In Rouen in '93 I destroyed $15,000 worth of manuscript, and in Paris in the beginning of '94, I destroyed $10,000 worth—I mean estimated as magazine stuff," he says in his autobiography, "I was afraid to keep those piles of manuscript on hand lest I be tempted to sell them, for I was fairly well persuaded that they were not up to standard." With old age and failing health, that margin of unpublishable waste grew to enormous proportions. Nevertheless Mark Twain went to his desk every day and wrote.

The death of his youngest daughter, Jean, in 1909 was the final blow; it killed what remained of his creative power. Too ill himself to attend the funeral that took place in a snowstorm at the old farm in Elmira, he sought refuge, for the last time, in writing. *The Death of Jean* was his farewell to his daughter—and to his art as well. "I shall never write anything any more," he told his friend, Albert Bigelow Paine. He never did.

A great public figure, a perennial after-dinner speaker and a witty companion, Mark Twain was in social demand to the last. Considered a popular humorist at the outset of his career, he was recognized during his late years as one of the greatest American fiction writers. Yale and Oxford gave honorary degrees to the boy from Missouri who never went to school after he was twelve. He died on April 21, 1910, just four months after his daughter. He was seventy-four years old.

Mark Twain's death brought a sense of personal sorrow to millions of people the world over. For he was one of the most human of writers. His books came straight out of his own personal experience and reflected his own personality, rugged, brave, manly and generous. Beneath the humorous facade he turned to the world, a great idealist was hidden. "Always do right," he admonished his fellow humans with a bitter smile. "This will please some and astonish the rest."

This is what Mark Twain himself did all his life long: he pleased and astonished. He spoke the truth as he saw it with a fearless honesty, an originality and a poetic feeling that make his books loved and admired.

FROM LIFE ON THE MISSISSIPPI BY MARK TWAIN

At the end of what seemed a tedious while, I had managed to pack my head full of islands, towns, bars, "points," and bends; and a curiously inanimate mass of lumber it was, too. However, inasmuch as I could shut my eyes and reel off a good long string of these names without leaving out more than ten miles of river in every fifty, I began to feel that I could take a boat down to New Orleans if I could make her skip those little gaps. But of course my complacency could hardly get start enough to lift my nose a trifle into the air, before Mr. Bixby would think of something to fetch it down again. One day he turned on me suddenly with this settler:

"What is the shape of Walnut Bend?"

He might as well have asked me my grandmother's opinion of protoplasm. I reflected respectfully, and then said I didn't know it had any particular shape. My gun-powdery chief went off with a bang, of course, and then went on loading and firing until he was out of adjectives.

I had learned long ago that he only carried just so many rounds of ammunition, and was sure to subside into a very placable and even remorseful old smooth-bore as soon as they were all gone. That word "old" is merely affectionate; he was not more than thirty-four. I waited. By and by he said:

"My boy, you've got to know the *shape* of the river perfectly. It is all there is left to steer by on a very dark night. Everything else is blotted out and gone. But mind you, it hasn't the same shape in the night that it has in the daytime."

"How on earth am I ever going to learn it, then?"

"How do you follow a hall at home in the dark? Because you know the shape of it. You can't see it."

"Do you mean to say that I've got to know all the million trifling variations of shape in the banks of this interminable river as well as I know the shape of the front hall at home?"

"On my honor, you've got to know them *better* than any man ever did know the shapes of the halls in his own house."

"I wish I was dead!"

"Now, I don't want to discourage you, but—"

"Well, pile it on me; I might as well have it now as another time."

"You see, this has got to be learned; there isn't any getting around it. A clear starlight night throws such heavy shadows that, if you didn't know the shape of a shore perfectly, you would claw away from every bunch of timber, because you would take the black shadow of it for a solid cape; and you see you would be getting scared to death every fifteen minutes by the watch. You would be fifty yards from shore all the time when you ought to be within fifty feet of it. You can't see a snag in one of those shadows, but you know exactly where it is, and the shape of the river tells you when you are coming to it. Then there's your pitch-dark night; the river is a very different shape on a pitch-dark night from what it is on a star-light night. All shores seem to be straight lines, then, and mighty dim ones, too; and you'd *run* them for straight lines, only you know better. You boldly drive your boat right into what seems to be a solid, straight wall (you knowing very well that in reality there is a curve there), and that wall falls back and makes way for you. Then there's your gray mist. You take a night when there's one of these grisly, drizzly, gray mists, and then there isn't *any* particular shape to a shore. A gray mist would tangle the head of the oldest man that ever lived. Well, then, different kinds of *moonlight* change the shape of the river in different ways. You see—"

"Oh, don't say any more, please! Have I got to learn the shape of the river according to all these five hundred thousand different ways? If I tried to carry all that cargo in my head it would make me stoop-shouldered."

"No! you only learn *the* shape of the river; and you learn it with such absolute certainty that you can always steer by the shape that's *in your head,* and never mind the one that's before your eyes."

"Very well, I'll try it; but, after I have learned it, can I depend on it? Will it keep the same form and not go fooling around?"

Before Mr. Bixby could answer, Mr. W. came in to take the watch, and he said:

"Bixby, you'll have to look out for President's Island, and all that country clear away up above the Old Hen and Chickens. The banks are caving and the shape of the shores changing like everything. Why, you wouldn't know the point above 40. You can go up inside the old sycamore snag, now."[1]

So that question was answered. Here were leagues of shore changing shape. My spirits were down in the mud again. Two things seemed pretty apparent to me. One was, that in order to be a pilot a man had got to learn more than any one man ought to be allowed to know; and the other was, that he must learn it all over again in a different way every twenty-four hours.

That night we had the watch until twelve. Now it was an ancient river custom for the two pilots to chat a bit when the watch changed. While the relieving pilot put on his gloves and lit his cigar, his partner, the retiring pilot, would say something like this:

[1] It may not be necessary, but still it can do no harm to explain that "inside" means between the snag and the shore.—M. T.

"I judge the upper bar is making down a little at Hale's Point; had quarter twain with the lower lead and mark twain[2] with the other."

"Yes, I thought it was making down a little, last trip. Meet any boats?"

"Met one abreast the head of 21, but she was away over hugging the bar, and I couldn't make her out entirely. I took her for the *Sunny South*—hadn't any skylights forward of the chimneys."

And so on. And as the relieving pilot took the wheel his partner[3] would mention that we were in such-and-such a bend, and say we were abreast of such-and-such a man's woodyard or plantation. This was courtesy; I supposed it was *necessity*. But Mr. W. came on watch full twelve minutes late on this particular night—a tremendous breach of etiquette; in fact, it is the unpardonable sin among pilots. So Mr. Bixby gave him no greeting whatever, but simply surrendered the wheel and marched out of the pilot-house without a word. I was appalled; it was a villainous night for blackness, we were in a particularly wide and blind part of the river, where there was no shape or substance to anything, and it seemed incredible that Mr. Bixby should have left that poor fellow to kill the boat, trying to find out where he was. But I resolved that I would stand by him anyway. He should find that he was not wholly friendless. So I stood around, and waited to be asked where we were. But Mr. W. plunged on serenely through the solid firmament of black cats that stood for an atmosphere, and never opened his mouth. "Here is a proud devil!" thought I; "here is a limb of Satan that would rather send us all to destruction than put himself under obligations to me, because I am not yet one of the salt of the earth and privileged to snub captains and lord it over everything dead and alive in a steamboat." I pres-

[2] Two fathoms. Quarter twain is 2¼ fathoms, 13½ feet. Mark three is three fathoms.

[3] "Partner" is technical for "the other pilot."

ently climbed up on the bench; I did not think it was safe to go to sleep while this lunatic was on watch.

However, I must have gone to sleep in the course of time because the next thing I was aware of was the fact that day was breaking, Mr. W. gone, and Mr. Bixby at the wheel again. So it was four o'clock and all well—but me; I felt like a skinful of dry bones, and all of them trying to ache at once.

Mr. Bixby asked me what I had stayed up there for. I confessed that it was to do Mr. W. a benevolence—tell him where he was. It took five minutes for the entire preposterousness of the thing to filter into Mr. Bixby's system, and then I judge it filled him nearly up to the chin; because he paid me a compliment—and not much of a one either. He said:

"Well, taking you by and large, you do seem to be more different kinds of an ass than any creature I ever saw before. What did you suppose he wanted to know for?"

I said I thought it might be a convenience to him.

"Convenience! D———nation! Didn't I tell you that a man's got to know the river in the night the same as he'd know his own front hall?"

"Well, I can follow the front hall in the dark if I know it *is* the front hall; but suppose you set me down in the middle of it in the dark and not tell me which hall it is; how am *I* to know?"

"Well, you've *got* to, on the river!"

"All right. Then I'm glad I never said anything to Mr. W."

"I should say so! Why, he'd have slammed you through the window and utterly ruined a hundred dollars' worth of window-sash and stuff."

I was glad this damage had been saved, for it would have made me unpopular with the owners. They always hated anybody who had the name of being careless and injuring things.

I went to work now to learn the shape of the river; and of all the eluding and ungraspable objects that ever I tried to get mind or hands on, that was the chief. I would fasten my eyes upon a sharp, wooded point that projected far into the river some miles ahead of me, and go to laboriously photographing its shape upon my brain; and just as I was beginning to succeed to my satisfaction, we would draw up toward it and the exasperating thing would begin to melt away and fold back into the bank! If there had been a conspicuous dead tree standing upon the very point of the cape, I would find that tree inconspicuously merged into the general forest, and occupying the middle of a straight shore, when I got abreast of it! No prominent hill would stick to its shape long enough for me to make up my mind what its form really was, but it was as dissolving and changeful as if it had been a mountain of butter in the hottest corner of the tropics. Nothing ever had the same shape when I was coming downstream that it had borne when I went up. I mentioned these little difficulties to Mr. Bixby. He said:

"That's the very main virtue of the thing. If the shapes didn't change every three seconds they wouldn't be of any use. Take this place where we are now, for instance. As long as that hill over yonder is only one hill, I can boom right along the way I'm going; but the moment it splits at the top and forms a V, I know I've got to scratch to starboard in a hurry, or I'll bang this boat's brains out against a rock; and then the moment one of the prongs of the V swings behind the other, I've got to waltz to larboard again, or I'll have a misunderstanding with a snag that would snatch the keelson out of this steamboat as neatly as if it were a sliver in your hand. If that hill didn't change its shape on bad nights there would be an awful steamboat graveyard around here inside of a year."

It was plain that I had got to learn the shape of the river in all the different ways that could be thought of—upside down, wrong end first, inside out, fore-and-aft, and "thortships"—and then know what to do on gray nights when it hadn't any shape at all. So I set about it. In the course of time I began to get the best of this knotty lesson, and my self-complacency moved to the front once more. Mr. Bixby was all fixed, and ready to start it to the rear again. He opened on me after this fashion:

"How much water did we have in the middle crossing at Hole-in-the-Wall, trip before last?"

I considered this an outrage. I said:

"Every trip, down and up, the leadsmen are singing through that tangled place for three-quarters of an hour on a stretch. How do you reckon I can remember such a mess as that?"

"My boy, you've got to remember it. You've got to remember the exact spot and the exact marks the boat lay in when we had the shoalest water, in every one of the five hundred shoal places between St. Louis and New Orleans; and you mustn't get the shoal soundings and marks of one trip mixed up with the shoal soundings and marks of another, either, for they're not often twice alike. You must keep them separate."

When I came to myself again, I said:

"When I get so that I can do that, I'll be able to raise the dead, and then I won't have to pilot a steamboat to make a living. I want to retire from this business. I want a slush-bucket and a brush; I'm only fit for a roustabout. I haven't got brains enough to be a pilot; and if I had I wouldn't have strength enough to carry them around, unless I went on crutches."

"Now drop that! When I say I'll learn[4] a man the river, I mean it. And you can depend on it, I'll learn him or kill him."

[4] "Teach" is not in the river vocabulary.

V ROBERT LOUIS STEVENSON
1850-1894

"An art is a fine fortune, a palace in a park, a band of music, health and physical beauty; all but love—to any worthy practiser. I sleep upon my art as a pillow; I waken in my art; I am unready for death because I hate to leave it. I love my wife . . . but while I can conceive of my being widowed, I refuse the offering of life without my art."

Robert Louis Stevenson was thirty-three years old when he wrote those words. At that time he was married to a woman he called "the best investment ever made by man"; he had devoted friends; he had tasted success. He was not a boy mouthing vague theory; he was a man speaking out of experience. For him writing was all important: the life in his life. "I *am* not but in my art; it is me," he says. "I am the body of it merely."

Stevenson was born in Edinburgh, Scotland, in 1850; he died in Samoa in 1894. He had a short life. Yet in those meager forty-four years of living he earned an enduring reputation as a writer. A master of English prose, he tried his hand at almost every kind of literary form. He wrote essays in a style that was almost perfect; he wrote tales of adventure full of incident and excitement; he wrote mediocre plays; he composed nursery verse that was touched with genius and adult verse of distinction; he wrote novels and short stories that ranged widely over the human scene. And he did all this under the handicap of constant ill health.

"I have written in bed and written out of it, written in hemorrhages, written in sickness, written torn by coughing, written when my head swam for weakness; and for so long it seems to me I have won my wager and recovered my glove," Stevenson wrote George Meredith only the year before he died. "Few are the days when I am not in some physical distress. And the battle goes on—ill or well is a trifle so as it goes."

Louis, as his family called him, was delicate from birth, and the harsh Scottish winters aggravated his constitutional weakness. As a child, he was sick most of the time. There were whole winters when he never stepped outside his parents' house. But, courageous and gay by nature, he made the best of a bad situation and used his active imagination to convert "the land of counterpane" that was his reality into the land of adventure he longed for. A cousin, who knew him well in those early days, says, "He was a very delicate child and not always fit to play with other children but he had a delightful and untiring companion always at hand—himself. He told himself stories: they were generally tales of adventure."

All his life long Robert Louis Stevenson longed for adventure and all his life long ill health denied it to him. But the lesson he had learned in childhood stood him in good stead. "It is quite possible and even comparatively easy," Stevenson wrote a friend from his sickbed in Switzerland, "so to enfold oneself in pleasant fancies, that the real ties of life may seem but as the white snow shower in the street, that only gives a relish to the swept hearth and the lively fire within. By such means I have forgotten hunger, I have sometimes eased pain, and I have invariably changed into the most pleasant hours of the day those very vacant and idle seasons which would otherwise have hung most heavily upon my mind." And by such means, Stevenson might have added, I have escaped from my sickbed existence into the adventurous and romantic life of *Treasure Island* and *Kidnapped.*

The writer J. M. Barrie, a fellow Scotsman, understood Stevenson's craving for adventure and the place it took in his life. "We all know," Barrie wrote, "that it is only in his books that Mr. Stevenson can live this life; see the brave bark riding joyously on the waves, the black flag, the dash of red color twisting around a mountainside. Alas! The drummer lies on a couch beating his drum."

There is no doubt that chronic ill health left its traces not only on Stevenson's writing but on his character as well. The delicate only child of hovering parents, he found it difficult to adjust to boys of his own age. Thin-armed and spindle-legged, more accustomed to telling himself stories than to playing games, the young Louis disliked the rough-and-tumble of school life and refused to take part in the snowball fights that were the staple schoolboy amusement during the long, cold Edinburgh winters. The other boys thought him odd. They called him "daft" or "dafty" and made him the butt of their pranks.

And in spite of a brilliant mind, Louis Stevenson was a poor student. Dreamy and undisciplined, he had a hungry appetite for reading and none at all for study. Often he solved his dislike for school by playing truant, a tactic which, for some peculiar reason, his father encouraged. And as the Edinburgh winter was poison to both Louis and his mother, they fled from it time and again, spending long happy months in the warm, sunny climate of southern France.

But, even at this time, the lazy, undisciplined Louis was a different person when it came to writing. From an early age he knew that he wanted to write and he trained himself for his chosen work with a strength of purpose and a discipline that was amazing. "Whenever a book or passage particularly pleased me, in which there was either some conscious force or some happy distinction of style," he said, "I must sit down at once and set myself to ape that quality. I was unsuccessful and I knew it; and tried again, and was again unsuccessful; and always unsuccessful. But at least in these vain bouts I got some practise in rhythm, in harmony, in construction, and in the coordination of part. I have thus played the sedulous ape to Hazlitt, to Lamb, to Wordsworth, to Sir Thomas Browne, to Defoe, to Hawthorne, to Montaigne, to Baudelaire and to Obermann—*that* like it or not, is the way to write."

Louis was a greedy reader. But he was so single-minded in his pursuit of his goal that he even harnessed this favorite pastime to his needs as an apprentice writer. He was willing to read slowly so that he could listen to each word. "Too many of us read by the eye," he declared, "but the man who means to write must, whether he articulates or not, read everything by the ear. In short as a musician reads a score and can hear harmony, so the literary man, even when skimming with the eye, must be able to hear the words uttered."

When Louis was seventeen the question of his future career first came up for serious discussion. Stevenson told his father that he wanted to be a writer, but so far he had produced nothing to justify this hope. At the age of six he had dictated a history of Moses to his mother and during his school years he had written some clumsy novels, a libretto called "The Baleful Potato" and "The Pentland Uprising: A Page of History." The latter work was by far the most promising, and the elder Stevenson, a doting father, paid to have it published. On reading the printed version, however, he judged it to be a youthful and unworthy piece of writing and, rather than allow his son's work to be exposed to public criticism, he bought back the whole edition almost as soon as it came off the press. This unsuccessful venture did not help matters. In any case Thomas Stevenson did not consider writing a "serious" or "reliable" profession and he refused to consider it as a career for his son. For generations Stevensons had been civil engineers; Louis could not do better than follow the family tradition.

Victorian parents believed wholeheartedly in the principle that "father knows best" and, if they could not win an argument by persuasion, they did not hesitate to apply financial pressure. So in the end Louis was forced to bow to his father's wishes and enroll in the engineering school of Edinburgh University.

Forced into a career that was not his by choice, Louis arrived at the University in a state of violent rebellion. He also disapproved of Victorian thought and morals, scorned the formal education that was offered him, and resented the authority of his professors. To show his disapproval of the university system in particular and of adult supervision in general, he cut his classes frequently. When, at the end of the term, he applied to one of his professors for a necessary certificate, that long-suffering educator refused to give it to him. "There may be doubtful cases but there is no doubt about yours," he said. "You simply have not attended classes."

Unpopular as Louis was with his professors, he was even more unpopular with his classmates. He refused to take part in their games, he was as rude as possible to everyone, and he affected an eccentric way of dressing.

"At that time Louis Stevenson was the queerest looking object you could conceive," a fellow classmate reports. "To begin with he was badly put together, a slithering, loose flail of a fellow, all joints, elbows and exposed spindle-shanks, his trousers being generally a foot too short in the leg. He was so like a scare-crow that one almost expected him to creak in the wind. And what struck us all was that he seemed to take pride in aggravating the oddities of nature. When the weather happened to be fine—and I don't remember seeing him when it wasn't—he came in a battered straw hat that his grandfather must have worn and laid aside because it was out of date. Under that antiquated headgear his long, lank hair fell straggling to his shoulders, giving him a look of a quack or gypsy. He wore duck trousers and a black shirt with a loose collar and a tie that might be a strip torn from a cast-away carpet. His jacket was of black velvet and it was noticeable that it never seemed good or new.

"As you may suppose, all this was matter for ridicule which we made no attempt to conceal: but his airs were even more ridiculous than his clothes. He seemed to make eccentricity a cult. He was always posing, always as the phrase went, showing off. We just laughed at him, dubbing him crank and humbug. He seemed not to care a straw; in fact he rather liked being the object of so much attention. The more we jeered and jibed the more he posed. Maybe it was defiance: I don't know. But if he had any feeling he must have been one of the most unhappy men who ever set foot on the old quadrangle. He had no friends that we could see."

Louis may have regretted his lack of friends but he was not as vulnerable to loneliness as other young men of his age. Constant illness had accustomed him to being alone, and also he was content to live in his art and to work toward his goal of becoming a writer. "All through my boyhood and youth," he tells us, "I was known and pointed out for the pattern of an idler and yet I was always busy on my own private end, which was to learn to write. I kept always two books in my pocket, one to read, one to write in. As I walked, my mind was busy fitting what I saw with appropriate words; when I sat by the roadside, I would either read, or a pencil and a penny version book would be in my hand to note down the features of the scene or commemorate some halting stanzas. Thus I lived with words. It was not so much that I wished to be an author (though I wished that, too) as I had vowed that I would learn to write."

Heedless and lazy where everything else was concerned, when it came to his writing Stevenson already had that "infinite capacity for taking pains" which is a mark of genius. All his energies were channeled into a single outlet. Later, when he was already famous, R.L.S. explained his success to his stepson: "I am not a man of any unusual talent; I started out with very moderate abilities. My success has been due to my really remarkable industry; to developing what I had in me to the extreme limit. When a man begins to sharpen one faculty and keeps on sharpening it with tireless perseverance, he can achieve wonders. Everybody knows it; it's a commonplace. And yet how rare it is to find anybody doing it—I mean to the uttermost as I did. What genius I had was for *work.*"

Because he thought it might prove helpful to his writing, Stevenson overcame his dislike of conviviality and joined the literary club of Edinburgh University, the well-known Speculative Society. Twice he served as its president. Here, at last, he met some kindred spirits and made some friends. With three of these literary young men he founded the *Edinburgh University Magazine* which died, as so many college magazines do, after only a few issues.

Stevenson's determination to be a writer had now reached a point where it was agony for him to devote time to other pursuits. At last he found the courage to tell his father that he would no longer go on with his engineering studies. Although the elder Stevenson was disappointed at his son's decision, he realized that Louis's poor health meant that he would probably never be strong enough to withstand the rigors of an engineer's life. Thomas Stevenson, however, still refused to allow his son to become a writer. After long discussion a compromise was reached: Louis was to study law.

Stevenson took his law studies lightly. He attended classes very irregularly and devoted the major part of his time to writing. At this time he began to emerge from the posings of his adolescent years. In the company of his friends he was developing into a brilliant talker. With Charles Baxter, a companion of his Speculative Society days, and with Bob Stevenson, an artist cousin, he spent long hours discussing art, religion and politics. And in 1873, while on a visit to cousins in England, Stevenson met two people who were to have an important influence on his life, Mrs. Sitwell and her husband-to-be, Sidney Colvin.

Thomas Stevenson had never relaxed his efforts to dissuade Louis from his determination to be a writer. This constant parental disapproval had its effect. There were times, now, when Louis began to doubt his own talent. He talked the situation over with Mrs. Sitwell, who urged him to persevere in his ambition. She also wrote Sidney Colvin about the "fine, young spirit" that had appeared on the scene and urged him to come and add his voice to hers. Colvin arrived and was so enthusiastic about the writing Louis showed him that he sent the younger man back to Edinburgh from his English visit believing in himself and more hopeful than ever of his future as a writer.

This support came at a time when it was badly needed. For added to the constant strain at home that was created by the career problem, Louis had shocked his parents by declaring himself an atheist. Mrs. Stevenson wept over her son's heresy but Thomas Stevenson, a strict Calvinist, was so unhappy he became physically ill.

Louis, too, was unhappy. It hurt him to see his parents suffering on his account; but he felt that short of denying his own words there was nothing he could do to right the situation. "The thunderbolt has fallen with a vengeance," he wrote Charles Baxter. "If it were not too late, I think I could find it in my heart to retract, but it is too late; and again, am I to live my whole life as one falsehood?"

The family atmosphere was now so charged with unhappiness and reproach that Louis's own health wilted under the strain. Flight seemed the only solution to the impasse; Louis decided to go to London and continue his law studies there. By the time he reached that city, however, he was so ill that he was forced to consult a doctor. The diagnosis was serious: complete nervous exhaustion, complicated by the threat of tuberculosis.

Ordered to take a prolonged rest in a mild climate, Louis was sent abroad by his worried parents. He chose to go to Menton, a small town in the south of France which he had known and loved as a boy. In the warm, sunny climate of Menton his health began slowly to improve. As soon as he was a little better, he set to work. When Colvin, who had become a close friend, came to visit him at the end of the winter, he had a sheaf of manuscripts to show him. Colvin promised to take some of the essays back to London with him and try to place them with magazines. When Louis reached London in the late spring on his way home, Colvin met him with the good news that two of his pieces had been accepted for publication, an essay on Victor Hugo in *Macmillan's* and "Ordered South" in Leslie Stephen's *Cornhill Magazine*. For the first time R.L.S. could call himself a professional writer.

In Edinburgh, absence and anxiety had mended the rift between Louis and his parents. Although he resumed his law studies, no one now objected to the fact that he was devoting the major part of his time and energy to writing.

Eager as he was to establish himself in his chosen career, Stevenson would not compromise where his art was concerned. When Colvin wrote that he could get him a contract for an essay a month, Stevenson, fearing that such a commitment would threaten the quality of his work, refused the offer. "Do you imagine I could ever write an essay a month, or promise an essay even every three months?" he wrote Colvin. "I would rather die than enter into any such an arrangement. The essays must fall from me, essay by essay, as they ripen."

As yet the general public had taken no notice of R.L.S., but other writers had already recognized the arrival of a new and distinguished talent. Stevenson was elected to membership in the Saville Club, the leading London literary club, and Leslie Stephen, on a visit to Edinburgh, introduced him to a fellow *Cornhill* contributor, the poet, W. E. Henley.

Henley had come to Edinburgh to be treated by the celebrated surgeon, Lister, for a tubercular ailment. Under threat of having his leg amputated, he had just written the famous poem, "Invictus." In a letter to Mrs. Sitwell, Stevenson told of their meeting: "Yesterday Leslie Stephen, who was down here for a lecture, called on me and took me up to see a poor fellow, a sort of poet who has written for him, and who has been eighteen months in our infirmary, and may be, for all I know, eighteen months more. It was very sad to see him there in a little room with two beds, and a couple of sick children in the other bed; a girl came in to visit the children, and played dominoes on the counterpane with them; the gas flared and crackled, the fire burned in a dull, economical way; Stephen and I sat on a couple of chairs and the poor fellow sat up in his bed with his hair and beard all tangled, and talked as cheerfully as if he had been in a King's palace, or the great King's palace of the blue air. I shall try to be of use to him."

Henley was a remarkable man. For many years he and Stevenson were of mutual use to each other. They had much in common. Both were writers, both were men of courage and gaiety, both were plagued by ill health. For both of them the new friendship proved stimulating and productive.

In July, 1875, Stevenson at last succeeded in passing his bar examinations. He had never wanted to be a lawyer and, although for a short period, to please his parents, he attended trials in wig and gown, he never practiced law. But his father had promised him a thousand pounds if he obtained his degree, and Louis now used that money to set off on a trip to France. For the next two years he visited Edinburgh only infrequently. "You shouldn't have had a tramp for a son," he told his mother on one of his short visits, and set off again for France.

In France he spent most of his time tramping through the countryside, and the fresh air and exercise made him healthier and happier than he had ever been before. His journeys supplied him with raw material for his writing. A canoe trip from Antwerp to Grez became *An Inland Voyage* and a journey through the Cévennes gave him the inspiration for *Travels with a Donkey*.

Both books were praised by the critics. But Stevenson felt that he should have done still better. "About criticism," he wrote his proud mother, "I was more surprised at the tone of the critics than I suppose anyone else. And the effect it has produced on me is one of shame. If they liked that so much, I ought to have given them something better. And I shall try to do so."

The forest of Fontainebleau was one of the places Stevenson liked best. Through Bob, the painter cousin, he was admitted to the artist colonies at Barbizon and Grez. Here, the young painters were struggling with an apprenticeship that paralleled his own. Their companionship was of immense benefit to Stevenson: "Let the young artist dwell much amongst his fellow-craftsmen," he wrote, "they alone can take a serious interest in the childish tasks and pitiful successes of these years. They alone can behold with equanimity this fingering of the dumb keyboard, this polishing of empty sentences, this dull and literal painting of dull and insignificant subjects."

Endlessly the young artists talked about their craft. "Art is first of all and last of all, a trade," Stevenson now declared. "The love of words and not a desire to publish new discoveries, the love of form and not a novel reading of historical events, mark the vocation of the writer. The artist first plays with his material as a child plays with a kaleidoscope; and he is already in a second stage when he begins to use his pretty counters for the end of representation. In that, he must pause long and faithfully; that is the end of apprenticeship; and it is only the few who will really go beyond it, and go forward fully equipped to do the business of real art—to give life to abstractions and charm to facts."

During this period, Bob was his cousin's favorite companion. When they were together they talked through the night, when they were apart they wrote each other long letters. "There is but one art—to omit!" Louis wrote Bob. "If I knew how to omit I would ask no other knowledge. A man who knew how to omit would make an *Iliad* of a daily paper. Artistic sight is judicious blindness." Stevenson became a past master in the art of omission. It was this inspired economy that made his style famous in later days for its clarity, its grace, its focus and its spare strength.

Until 1876 the artist colonies of Fontainebleau forest were bachelor gatherings. Suddenly the word went round that two women had invaded the sacred precincts of Grez. "It is the beginning of the end," Stevenson sighed when he heard the news. He spoke more truly than he knew, for one of the women was to change his life.

Walking into the living room of the inn at Grez one evening, Stevenson saw a short, stocky American woman with dark hair, dark eyes and a strong chin, sitting with a group of the habitués. With her were her daughter and her son, Lloyd Osbourne, who later wrote this picture of Stevenson at twenty-seven: "He was tall and slight, with light brown hair, a small golden mustache and a ruddy complexion: and so gay and buoyant that he kept everyone in fits of laughter. He and his friends were under the spell of the *vie de bohème,* they wanted to be poor, improvident and reckless; they were eager to assert that they were outcasts and rebels. It was their custom to rail at the respectable and well-to-do. R.L.S.'s favorite expression was 'a common banker' used as one might refer to 'a common laborer.' "

Fanny Osbourne looked sad and romantic, sitting amidst the gay young bohemians. She was thirty-seven and married to an irresponsible man whose philanderings were notorious. She had come to France with her children to study art, and only a few weeks previously her youngest son had died in Paris. There was always something of the knight-errant in Stevenson's make-up. Mrs. Osbourne's sadness appealed to his chivalry as much as her dark good looks attracted him. By the end of the summer they were very much in love.

Life seemed, however, to have placed every possible obstacle between them. Mrs. Osbourne was still married, and the time for her return to America was at hand. Neither she nor Stevenson had any money. Stevenson went to London to see her off, and they said a sad good-by. But R.L.S. never lacked courage. He vowed that he would set to work and earn the money he needed to support a wife. "What a man truly wants, that he will get," he said, "or he will be changed in the trying."

After some months in America, Mrs. Osbourne decided to get a divorce. But the difficulties and worries this step entailed undermined her health so that she fell seriously ill. Stevenson was determined to join her at once. Knowing that his parents would oppose the marriage of their only son to a woman eleven years older and a divorcée besides, he felt that it would be unfair to ask his father for financial help. His writing would have to supply him with the funds he needed.

Only Henley and Colvin were told of his plan. Both did their best to dissuade their friend from an adventure they thought not only unwise but dangerous for a man in his delicate health. But Stevenson was determined to go to Fanny Osbourne, even if it killed him.

It nearly did. The trip across the Atlantic in the cheapest quarters of a small, crowded ship was arduous enough; but the journey to San Francisco by emigrant train was a nightmare. Stevenson's health went from bad to worse; his spirit, however, remained undefeated. "No man is any use until he has dared everything," he wrote Sidney Colvin from the train that took eleven days to cross the continent. "I feel just now as if I had, and so might become a man. 'If you have faith like a grain of mustard seed!' That is so true! Just now I have faith as big as a cigar case. I will not say die, and do not fear man nor fortune."

The rough San Francisco climate proved to be bad for Stevenson's health, so he visited Monterey, in the hope that an outdoor life might help him to regain the strength he had lost on the long journey. But almost immediately he fell ill with pleurisy and was found lying unconscious under a tree by two men who owned a nearby goat ranch. They took the sick stranger home with them and nursed him back to a degree of health. The attack of pleurisy, however, left Stevenson weak and in need of rest. But he desperately needed money. So he overworked and, in order to cut expenses, ate only one meal a day. This regime lasted exactly four months; then his health broke down completely. This time his illness was diagnosed as galloping consumption, and he was expected to die. Fanny Osbourne, who had by this time obtained her divorce, took him into her house and nursed him devotedly. At last he was told that he was out of immediate danger, and he and Fanny decided to get married at once. On his wedding day, May 19, 1880, Stevenson, as he himself put it, was still "a mere complication of coughs and bones."

Meanwhile Colvin had told the older Stevensons of their son's illness and of his determination to marry Fanny Osbourne. They wired Louis, not only a warm welcome to their new daughter-in-law, but also the financial help he needed so badly. It was characteristic of Stevenson that the first use he made of this money was to recall a manuscript he had been driven by financial need to sell before he was completely satisfied with it. *The Amateur Emigrant,* as the piece was called, had been written, as Stevenson himself said, "in a circle of hell unknown to Dante—that of the penniless and dying author." In this essay Stevenson had described his journey by emigrant train, making use of material that was still too fresh to have been properly assimilated. "I cannot describe a thing that is before me at the moment, or that has been before me only a little while before," Stevenson told Colvin. "I must allow my recollections to get thoroughly strained free from all the chaff till nothing is left except the pure gold; allow my memory to choose out what is truly memorable by a process of natural selection; and I piously believe that in this way I ensure the Survival of the Fittest."

After months of estrangement, it was a joy to Stevenson to know that the family peace was restored. Grateful to his father for his financial support ("I always light on my feet," he joked, "and the best part of my legs is my father"), Louis would have liked to sail for home at once. But he was still too weak to travel. So, with his wife and stepson, he spent some weeks recuperating in a deserted mining camp at Silverado, high in the mountains north of San Francisco. By midsummer he was well enough to travel. On the 7th of August, exactly a year after he left England, he sailed home with his wife and stepson.

It had been a desperate year and it left an indelible mark. As Henley wrote, "There were two Stevensons; the Stevenson who went to America in '79 and the Stevenson who came back." The close brush with death, the legacy of weakness it left behind and the responsibilities of marriage had sobered the "old, riotous, intrepid Louis" of bachelor days. Yet the American adventure, so disastrous to his health, provided Stevenson with valuable material that he used at a later date in writing *The Amateur Emigrant, Across the Plains, The Silverado Squatters* and many short stories.

Although, for the moment, the critical phase of Stevenson's illness had been surmounted, he was still ill with tuberculosis. And for the next ten years he went from place to place in a desperate quest for health. He tried the Alpine air at Davos, the sunny Riviera, the mild climate of southern England. Nothing helped. He would struggle back painfully to a fragile convalescence after each new attack of illness, then a fresh hemorrhage would again return him to his bed. The amazing fact is that he never stopped writing.

"It is plain that what enabled him to hold death at bay till 44," his stepson, Lloyd Osbourne, writes, "while so many of his generation with the same disease, and infinitely less impaired, succumbed long before him was: first this tremendous prepossession for his work, and secondly his invincible refusal to become an invalid."

A man who knew Stevenson during his Davos days gives a picture of R.L.S. that shows his determination to resist invalidism: "One knew at once he was, in Davosian parlance, 'lungy,' more 'lungy' even than the majority, but though so obviously a member of the crock company, he would, whenever he had an ounce of energy to spare, insist upon a place with the robust brigade. The latter were doing their tobogganing in the early morning, and with them, often enough, went Stevenson. I have a most vivid recollection of a first view of him homeward bound from one of these before-breakfast expeditions. He was dragging himself wearily along, towing a toboggan at his heels, his narrow, hunched-up figure cut clear against the surprising brilliance of the Davos world. With that pathetic, half-broken figure making so dominant a note in one's recollections, one marvels at the fortitude that made possible his later achievement."

After two years at Davos, Stevenson's health showed little improvement. Because he hated the sickroom atmosphere of that place, with its rows of sanatoriums and its population of invalids, he decided to move to the south of France. At Hyeres, the Stevensons found a charming chalet, and for a time the new environment seemed to be beneficial. Stevenson always referred to this period as "the happiest time in my life." His work was going well and *Treasure Island,* which had just come out in book form, had become an immediate "best seller." For the first time it was not only the critics who were applauding Stevenson's work!

Ever since his marriage, Stevenson had been largely dependent on his father for financial support. The popularity of *Treasure Island,* combined with what seemed like improved health, brought the hope of a more dignified way of living.

"Really, with such cause for gladness, I have not the heart to be dispirited by anything," he wrote his parents. "My child's verse book is finished; *Silverado* is due, too, and cast upon the waters; and this novel [*Prince Otto*] so near completion, it does look as if I should support myself with no trouble in the future. If I have only health, I can, I thank God. It is dreadful to be a great, big man and not be able to buy bread. . . .

"O that this may last!"

Unfortunately, it did not last. In 1884 Stevenson was again critically ill. Once more he fought off death. Again he turned to his writing but he was so weak now that he could only work "in little sittings." He suffered under the knowledge that no writer can do his best work under such conditions. "If I had with my present knowledge, twelve months of my old health," he wrote Edmund Gosse, "I would, could and should do something neat. As it is I have to tinker at my things in little sittings. . . . Well, I do not complain, but I do envy strong health where it is squandered, and may you never learn by experience the profound ennui and irritation of the shelved artist. For then, what is life? All that one has done to make one's life effective then doubles the itch of inefficiency."

In 1884 Stevenson had a new blow. His father, who had for so long been a bulwark of strength, began to fail in health. In order to be closer to him, Louis moved with his family to Bournemouth in the south of England. The Stevensons remained there for three years, and during most of that time Louis' health was so frail that he was virtually a prisoner in his own house. "Never was he so spectral, so emaciated, so unkempt and tragic a figure," writes Lloyd Osbourne. "His long hair, his eyes so abnormally brilliant in his wasted face, his sickroom garb, picked up at random and to which he gave no thought."

Yet, even during this dark time, Stevenson went on producing. *Kidnapped* and *Dr. Jekyll and Mr. Hyde* were both written at Bournemouth. Stevenson locked himself in his room for three days while he was writing the latter story. At the end of that time he emerged from his lair, gaunt, exhausted, but triumphant. That night he read the manuscript aloud to his wife and stepson. Mrs. Stevenson felt that the allegory missed fire and, as a result, what should have been a masterpiece was merely a good story.

The criticism hurt Stevenson. He flared up angrily, stormed

out of the room, and retreated upstairs. Mrs. Stevenson sat on unhappily beside the fire.

Suddenly Louis was back again. "You are right," he said, "I have absolutely missed the allegory, which after all is the whole point of the story." And before his horrified wife could stop him, he had thrown the manuscript into the fire.

Mrs. Stevenson was in tears. It was a drastic step but the artist in Louis knew that he could not do otherwise. "It was all wrong," he said, "and in trying to save some of it, I should have got hopelessly off the track. The only way was to put temptation beyond my reach." The "only way," perhaps, but also the hard way.

Three days later, the story was completely rewritten. 64,000 words in six days! A big output for a writer who was well; an almost incredible feat for a man in Stevenson's weak health. The reward came in due course: *Dr. Jekyll and Mr. Hyde* achieved world-wide fame and unanimous critical acclaim.

In 1887 Thomas Stevenson died, and Louis, depressed by the miserable Bournemouth years, determined to make a complete change in his way of living. Accompanied this time by his wife, his mother and his stepson, he sailed for America again.

This time he stepped off his ship in New York and found himself a celebrity. The unknown writer of 1879 had become the famous R.L.S. of 1887. The lobby of his hotel was crowded with callers; he was headlined, photographed and lionized. The new status was pleasant, but exhausting. Fame brought him a high price for his work: he was offered $8,000 for the American serial rights to his next story. For the rest of his life R.L.S. had as much money as he needed.

Stevenson spent the following winter at Saranac Lake, where Dr. Trudeau had started his center for tuberculosis patients. Physically, the life at Saranac proved beneficial, but Stevenson was saddened by a quarrel with Henley that ended this long, and productive friendship. Stevenson became melancholy and was now anxious to go "some place, any place."

Meanwhile, his wife, who had gone alone to San Francisco to visit relatives, heard of a seagoing yacht that was being offered for immediate charter. Feeling that her husband needed a change and knowing that sea air had always helped him in the past, she sent him a telegram. "Can secure splendid seagoing yacht *Casco* for $750 a month with most comfortable accommodation for six aft and six forward. Can be ready for sea in ten days. Reply immediately."

Stevenson was ready: "Blessed girl, take the yacht," he wired, "and expect us in ten days."

So, quite by chance, the whole family embarked on a pleasure jaunt that was planned to last only a few months. The *Casco* cruised among the little-known islands of the Pacific. And when the time arrived for the yacht to go home, Stevenson was not ready to go with her. With his family he booked passage on a small trading schooner and set out for islands that were still more remote. At Apia, on the island of Upolu, the Stevensons at last left ship. After two months they were so much attached to the beautiful wooded island and the friendly people who lived there that they decided to settle among them permanently.

Stevenson bought a tract of land and built himself a house. "I am now the owner of an estate," he wrote a friend in England, "upon Upolu, some two or three miles behind and above Apia. Three streams, two waterfalls, a great cliff, an ancient fort, a view of the seas and lowlands (or to be more precise) several views of them in various directions, all now are mine. Besides all this there is a great deal more forest than I have need for; or to be plain the whole estate is one impassable jungle, which must be cut down and through at considerable expense."

Ground was cleared and a cottage built. Later the original building was enlarged into a sizable two-story house with a red roof and a deep veranda. In a country where most of the dwellings were either huts or cottages, the new house, which the Stevensons christened Vailima ("three streams," in Samoan), looked like a palace.

The warm climate and the outdoor life brought about an almost miraculous improvement in Stevenson's health. For the first time in his life he was able to lead a comparatively normal existence. "I have now been some twenty months in the South Seas," he wrote his old Bournemouth doctor, "and am (up to date) a person whom you would scarcely know. I think nothing of long walks and rides; I was four and a half hours gone the other day, partly riding, partly climbing up a steep ravine." For someone who had spent most of his days indoors, when not actually confined to his bed, the new, free existence was a liberation. At times Stevenson chafed at his voluntary exile but he never seriously considered going back to the old invalid life.

Samoan politics were in a state of turmoil, and R.L.S. threw himself ardently into the fray. The Samoans looked up to him with admiration and affection and called him *Tusitala,* the teller of tales. They felt that he was truly their friend and, in order to show their gratitude, they insisted on building a road from his house to the point where his path joined the public road.

"Louis tried to put them off, not wishing to take them at their word," Stevenson's mother reports, "but they insisted on their offer. He proposed then that he should feed them while they were at work; but even this they refused, saying they wished to do it all themselves, as a *mea-alofa* (gift of love) to Tusitala, who had always been the

Samoans' friend." When the road was finished, Stevenson gave a big feast for the men who had built it, and it was solemnly christened "The Road of The Loving Heart."

Although Vailima was situated on a remote island, quite a few travelers came to visit Stevenson. He was glad to see new faces and entertained his guests in a feudal way. "After a chat 'tiffin' was announced," one visitor says, "and we all adjourned to the great, dark, panelled hall. As the guests were numerous, it was rather a tight pack around the table; however at last all were settled and the bright native boys, clad in Stuart tartan lava-lavas, handed around a quaint but delightful selection of American and native dishes."

Cloak-and-dagger politics, native boys in tartan lava-lavas, a lush and romantically beautiful island, all this was to the Stevenson taste. As Henry James remarked, "He was a romantic in an age of realism." At Vailima he had found a setting that suited his nature. But writing was still his reason for living.

To it he gave the best part of his day. He rose early, working in a small den upstairs rather than in the big library. "I don't write in the library, it's all so suitable for a literary man," Stevenson laughingly told a friend, "it puts every idea out of my head. I like a little den with nothing to distract me—a deal kitchen table and a couple of chairs—but the latter are really mere luxuries—quite unnecessary. I have lived in every sort of place, and find that a mat on the ground is as comfortable as anything. Breakfast is brought to me at five, but I have often done an hour's work before that."

Stevenson was famous now. Letters came to him from admirers the world over. Through lack of time and lack of strength, much of this correspondence had to remain unanswered. But Stevenson was never too busy to give help and advice to younger colleagues. To them he gave unstintingly. The following letter was written to a young painter, headed:

NOTES FOR THE STUDENT OF ANY ART

1. Keep an intelligent eye upon all the other arts. It is only by doing so that you come to see what Art is. Art is the end common to them all; it is none of the points by which they differ.

2. In this age beware of realism.

3. In your own art, bow your head over technique. Think of technique when you rise and when you go to bed. Forget purposes in the meanwhile; get to live technical processes, to glory in technical success; get to see the world entirely in terms of what you can do. Then when you have anything to say, the language will be apt and copious.

4. See the good in other peoples' work; it will never be yours. See the bad in your own, and don't cry about it; it will be there always. Try to use your faults; at any rate to use your knowledge of them, and don't run your head against stone walls. Art is not theology; nothing is forced. You have to represent with pleasure and effect, and the only way to find out what that is is by technical enterprise.

Stevenson looked at his own work with a critical eye. "A certain warmth (tepid enough) and a certain dash of the picturesque are my poor essential qualities," he said, "and if I went fooling after the too classical, I might even lose these."

A "dash of the picturesque" *was* one of Stevenson's essential qualities, but its use to the exclusion of the more human side of life was due to other causes. Confined to a sickroom for years, Stevenson had been deprived of the contact with both ordinary people and ordinary problems which serves as the raw material for normal writers. To compensate for this lack, he had been forced to substitute the romantic and the picturesque. As a result he felt that he was something of a "literary cherub—a head and a pair of wings with nothing to sit down on." In Samoa he was at last set free from his sickroom life. He could talk with all sorts of people, with the missionaries, the consular officials and the sailors who came ashore from visiting ships; he could also talk to the Samoans, all the way from the chiefs to his own servants. It was a return to the world.

Weir of Hermiston, Stevenson's last novel, reflected the new, free life of its author. It is a warm and profoundly human book. The "literary cherub" had grown into a man of genius. At Stevenson's death this last novel was still unfinished, but even in its incomplete state the critics were unanimous in calling it his masterpiece.

Strangely enough, Stevenson never appeared to be as well as during the last months of his life. He spent most of that final day dictating *Weir of Hermiston* to his stepdaughter, who had joined the family in Samoa to act as secretary. The work went so well that Stevenson decided to turn the evening meal into a celebration and at sundown he went to the cellar to get a bottle of burgundy. A little later, when he was helping his wife to make some mayonnaise for the feast, he suddenly collapsed.

A doctor came but he could do nothing. Stevenson was suffering from a blood clot on the brain. A bed was moved into the Great Hall, and the Samoan servants sat in a semicircle beside their unconscious master. Some kneeled on one knee so as to be ready to run should their beloved Tusitala need anything.

The family gathered around his bed. "We were watching dear Lou," writes Stevenson's mother. "Fanny and I were rubbing his arms with brandy and his shirt sleeves were pushed up, and showed their thinness; someone make a remark about his writing and the doctor said, 'How can anybody write books with arms like these?'

"I don't think I was ever so deeply impressed with the greatness of the struggle that my beloved child had made against his bad health. He had written at the rate of a volume a year for the last twenty years, in spite of weakness which most people would have looked on as an excuse for invalidism . . . and he lived, too, and loved his life."

Stevenson had expressed the wish to be buried on the summit of Mount Vaea. There was no path up that mountain so his native friends worked through the night to build one. That afternoon a dozen tall Samoans carried the coffin up the steep, difficult ascent. They made it a point of honor to carry their heavy load shoulder high all the way.

On Stevenson's simple tomb are engraved the words he himself wrote:

Under the wide and starry sky
Dig the grave and let me lie.
Glad did I live and gladly die,
And I laid me down with a will.

This be the verse you grave for me:
Here he lies where he longed to be;
Home is the sailor, home from sea,
And the hunter home from the hill.

From WEIR OF HERMISTON by Robert Louis Stevenson

[For the setting of his last novel, *Weir of Hermiston,* Stevenson, the Samoan exile, returned to the moorlands of the Scotland he knew and loved so well. "It is a singular thing that I should live here in the South Seas under conditions so new and so startling," he wrote his fellow Scot and fellow writer, J. M. Barrie, "and yet my imagination so continually inhabits the cold old huddle of grey hills from which we come." From Scottish history, too, came the character of the stern Lord Justice-Clerk who is the hero of *Weir of Hermiston.*

For Adam Weir is modeled on Lord Braxfield who, at his death in 1799, was known as the "Hanging Judge."

The tragedy of this austere and domineering man who was trapped in a conflict between his public duty and his private affections, had long ago caught Stevenson's imagination and had been slowly germinating in his subconscious mind. "I am still a 'slow study', and sit for a long while silent on my eggs," he wrote a friend. "Unconscious thought, there is the only method: macerate your subject, let it boil slowly, then take the lid off and look in—and there your stuff is—good or bad."

It was not till 1892 that Stevenson finally "took the lid off" the story that had been "macerating" in his subconscious mind for so long. From the first the novel went well. "I expect *The Justice Clerk* to be my masterpiece," he wrote. "My Braxfield is already a thing of beauty and a joy for ever." Writers are not always the best judges of their own work but in Stevenson's case, critical opinion has endorsed the author's verdict. *Weir of Hermiston* is Stevenson's masterpiece; the tragedy is that it had to remain unfinished:

In Edinburgh, toward the end of the 18th century, there lived a new Lord Justice-Clerk, Adam Weir. A stern and domineering man, he "looked rather to obedience than to duty" in choosing a wife. He was already forty when he married Jean Rutherford, a descendant of the "riding Rutherfords of Hermiston." Jean, a "pious, anxious, tender, tearful and incompetent woman," admired her austere and distinguished husband but suffered under his domineering and inconsiderate treatment of her. Her only joy was her son, Archie, a handsome child who inherited his mother's sensitive nature and his father's pugnacity.

When her son was still a small boy, Mrs. Weir died, and Archie lived alone in Edinburgh with his stern father. The Lord Justice-Clerk saw very little of his son. But every evening after dinner, at a given signal, Archie was brought to his father for a few minutes, "given nuts and a glass of port, regarded sardonically, questioned sarcastically." Small wonder that Archie grew up to be serious, brilliant and shy. Like other Edinburgh boys he graduated from school to the university where he studied law, shone in the debating club, the famous Speculative Society, but took little part in undergraduate life. In fact he was so introverted that when Frank Innes, a classmate, was asked if he was a friend of Archie Weir's, he answered, "I know Weir but I never met Archie."

One day in 1813, Archie, out of curiosity, wandered into his father's courtroom. The Lord Justice-Clerk was trying a criminal case, and Archie was shocked at the scornful brutality and almost "savage pleasure" with which his father sentenced the culprit to be hanged.

Haunted by the pitiful case, Archie went, on the morning of the execution, to watch the hanging. Horrified and disgusted by what he had seen, he shouted out a denunciation of capital punishment which, under the circumstances, amounted also to a denunciation of his father. That evening he compounded his disloyalty by making an impassioned speech against capital punishment at a meeting of the Speculative Society.

In due course the Lord Justice-Clerk heard of his son's betrayal. In his strange, aloof, silent way he had loved his son, and Archie's disloyalty wounded him deeply. Cruel, stern, but with a certain nobility where his office was concerned, he was convinced that no man was fitted to be a lawyer if he disapproved of capital punishment, which was a part of Scottish Law. He told Archie that he must give up his legal studies and be exiled to the country where he was to live and work and be the laird of Hermiston.

Archie accepted his father's sentence. Resigning from the university, he set off for Hermiston:]

The road to Hermiston runs for a great part of the way up the valley of a stream, a favorite with anglers and with midges, full of falls and pools, and shaded by willows and natural woods of birch. Here and there, but at great distances, a byway branches off, and a gaunt farmhouse may be descried above in a fold of the hill; but the more part of the time, the road would be quite empty of passage and the hills of habitation. Hermiston parish is one of the least populous in Scotland; and by the time you came that length, you would scarce be surprised at the inimitable smallness of the kirk, a dwarfish, ancient place seated for fifty, and standing in a green by the burn-side among two-score grave-stones. The manse close by, although no more than a cottage, is surrounded by the brightness of a flower-garden and the straw roofs of bees; and the whole colony, kirk and manse, garden and graveyard, finds harbourage in a grove of rowans, and is all the year round in a great silence broken only by the drone of the bees, the tinkle of the burn, and the bell on Sundays. A mile beyond the kirk the road leaves the valley by a precipitous ascent, and brings you a little after to the place of Hermiston, where it comes to an end in the backyard before the coach-house. All beyond and about is the great field of the hills; the plover, the curlew, and the lark cry there; the wind blows as it blows in a ship's rigging, hard and cold and pure; and the hill-tops huddle one behind another like a herd of cattle into the sunset.

The house was sixty years old, unsightly, comfortable; a farmyard and a kitchen garden on the left, with a fruit wall where little hard green pears came to their maturity about the end of October.

The policy (as who should say the park) was of some extent, but very ill reclaimed; heather and moorfowl had crossed the boundary wall and spread and roosted within; and it would have tasked a landscape gardener to say where policy ended and unpolicied nature began. My lord had been led by the influence of Mr. Sheriff Scott into a considerable design of planting; many acres were accordingly set out with fir, and the little feathery besoms gave a false scale and lent a strange air of a toy-shop in the moors. A great, rooty sweetness of bogs was in the air, and at all seasons an infinite melancholy piping of hill birds. Standing so high and with so little shelter, it was a cold, exposed house, splashed by showers, drenched by continuous rains that made the gutters to spout, beaten upon and buffeted by all the winds of heaven; and the prospect would be often black with tempest, and often white with the snows of winter. But the house was wind and weather proof, the hearths were kept bright and the rooms pleasant with live fires of peat; and Archie might sit of an evening and hear the squalls bugle on the moorland, and watch the fire prosper in the earthy fuel, and the smoke winding up the chimney, and drink deep of the pleasures of shelter.

Solitary as the place was, Archie did not want neighbors. Every night, if he chose, he might go down to the manse and share a "brewst" of toddy with the minister—a hare-brained ancient gentleman, long and light and still active, though his knees were loosened with age, and his voice broke continually in childish trebles—and his lady wife, a heavy, comely dame, without a word to say for herself beyond good even and good day. Harum-scarum, clodpole young lairds of the neighborhood paid him the compliment of a visit. Young Hay of Romanes rode down to call on his crop-eared pony; young Pringle of Drumanno came up on his bony grey. Hay remained on the hospitable field, and must be carried to bed; Pringle got somehow to his saddle about 3 A.M., and (as Archie stood with the lamp on the upper doorstep) lurched, uttered a senseless view-halloa, and vanished out of the small circle of illumination like a wraith. Yet a minute or two longer the clatter of his break-neck flight was audible, then it was cut off by the intervening steepness of the hill; and again, a great while after, the renewed beating of phantom horse-hoofs, far in the valley of the Hermiston, showed that the horse at least, if not his rider, was still on the homeward way.

There was a Tuesday club at the "Cross-keys" in Crossmichael, where the young bloods of the country-side congregated and drank deep on a percentage of the expense, so that he was left gainer who should have drunk the most. Archie had no great mind to this diversion, but he took it like a duty laid upon him, went with a decent regularity, did his manfullest with the liquor, held up his head in local jests, and got home again and was able to put up his horse, to the admiration of Kirstie [his housekeeper] and the lass that helped her. He dined at Driffel, supped at Windielaws. He went to the new year's ball at Huntsfield and was made welcome, and thereafter rode to hounds with my Lord Muirfell, upon whose name, as that of a legitimate Lord of Parliament, in a work so full of Lords of Session, my pen should pause reverently. Yet the same fate attended him here as in Edinburgh. The habit of solitude tends to perpetuate itself, and an austerity of which he was quite unconscious, and a pride which seemed arrogance, and perhaps was chiefly shyness, discouraged and offended his new companions. Hay did not return more than twice, Pringle never at all, and there came a time when Archie even desisted from the Tuesday Club, and became in all things—what he had had the name of almost from the first—the Recluse of Hermiston. High-nosed Miss Pringle of Drumanno and high-stepping Miss Marshall of the Mains were understood to have had a difference of opinion about him the day after the ball—he was none the wiser, he could not suppose himself to be remarked by these entrancing ladies. At the ball itself my Lord Muirfell's daughter, the Lady Flora, spoke to him twice, and the second time with a touch of appeal, so that her colour rose and her voice trembled a little in his ear, like a passive grace in music. He stepped back with a heart on fire, coldly and not ungracefully excused himself, and a little after watched her dancing with young Drumanno of the empty laugh, and was harrowed at the sight, and raged to himself that this was a world in which it was given to Drumanno to please, and to himself only to stand aside and envy. He seemed excluded, as of right, from favor of such society—seemed to extinguish mirth wherever he came, and was quick to feel the wound, and desist and retire into solitude. If he had but understood the figure he presented, and the impression he made on these bright eyes and tender hearts; if he had but guessed that the Recluse of Hermiston, young, graceful, well-spoken, but always cold, stirred the maidens of the country with the charm of Byronism when Byronism was new, it may be questioned whether his destiny might not even yet have been modified. It may be questioned, and I think it should be doubted. It was in his horoscope to be parsimonious of pain to himself, or of the chance of pain, even to the avoidance of any opportunity of pleasure; to have a Roman sense of duty, an instinctive aristocracy of manners and taste; to be the son of Adam Weir and Jean Rutherford.